THE STATE MAKERS
Builders of the Nation

by BILL and SUE SEVERN

Here are the stories of fifty men who had a leading part in America's greatest adventure, the building of the nation, block by block, into the United States. They are the state makers, some of them little known outside the states they helped to create.

Included among the men from the thirteen original states are Thomas Mifflin of Pennsylvania, Alexander Hamilton of New York, and Charles Pinckney of South Carolina. As the nation moves westward, we meet Ohio's Thomas Worthington, Indiana's William H. Harrison, Illinois' Jesse Thomas, as well as Sam Houston of Texas and Bennet Riley of California, and as one of our newest states enters the Union, Ernest Gruening of Alaska. Each state, of course, could claim many others among its builders, since no one man ever created a state by himself. But these are some of the men who led their neighbors in the building of our government by the people.

Our states all grew in different ways. Some were born in protest, some in battle, others almost by chance, and some struggled to be included in the Union against the will of a nation reluctant to have them at the time.

The state makers also were each different in character. Some were bold fighters and others were calm planners. Some were men of strong personal ambition, while others were selfless in devotion to a cause. But whatever else, all were adventurers.

THE
STATE
MAKERS

Bill and Sue Severn

G. P. PUTNAM'S SONS

NEW YORK

Published simultaneously in the Dominion of
Canada by Longmans Canada Limited, Toronto

Library of Congress Catalog Card Number 63–7756

Manufactured in the United States of America

10214

Second Impression

CONTENTS

Foreword

PART I: THE FIRST THIRTEEN

PART II: ACROSS THE MOUNTAINS

5

24991

PART III: SPREADING OUT THE NATION

PART IV: BATTLES AND BOUNDARIES

PART V: THE SECOND CENTURY

FOREWORD

Here are the stories of fifty men who had a leading part in America's greatest adventure, the building of the nation, block by block, into these United States.

They are the state makers, some of them little known outside the states they helped to make. Each state, of course, could claim many others among its builders, since no one man ever created a state by himself. But these are some of the men who led their neighbors in the building of our government by the people.

Our states all grew in different ways. Some were born in protest, some in battle, others almost by chance, and some struggled to be included in the Union against the will of a nation reluctant to have them at the time.

The state makers also were each different in character. Some were bold fighters, others calm planners, many were men of strong personal ambition, and some were selfless in devotion to a cause. But, whatever else, all were adventurers.

PART I. THE FIRST THIRTEEN

DELAWARE

Motto: Liberty and Independence

Flower: Peach Blossom   Bird: Blue Hen Chicken

Tree: American Holly

Admitted to the Union: 1787

☆

Years before there was any thought of a United States, the people of Delaware wanted an independent government. They had good reason because, almost from the time Henry Hudson discovered Delaware Bay in 1609, nations and men battled over who should rule the area.

Dutch colonists came first and were killed by the Indians. Peter Minuit led a Swedish expedition to Wilmington in 1638 and established the first permanent settlement on Delaware soil. The Dutch, the Swedes, and then the English made claims to the area.

Under William Penn, Delaware became the Three Lower Counties of Pennsylvania. After disputes with Penn, the counties were granted a form of self-rule, although still not full independence as a Crown colony.

The settlers gradually took more rights to themselves, and in 1751 a seal was adopted containing the arms of the King of Great Britain and "Counties on Delaware." By 1765, when delegates from the colonies met in New York to protest English colonial taxes, Delaware demanded an equal vote as a government.

A convention of delegates of the Three Counties met at New Castle in 1776 and framed a constitution for "the Delaware State." Delaware was the first state to ratify the new Constitution of the United States on December 7, 1787.

CAESAR RODNEY
(1728–1783)

"Caesar Rodney is the oddest-looking man in the world," John Adams once wrote in his diary. "He is tall, thin, slender as a reed, pale. His face is not bigger than a large apple. Yet, there is sense and fire, spirit, wit and humor in his countenance."

Rodney, a leader of Delaware's fight for independence, helped bring it to statehood through the troubled years of revolution. As a patriot soldier, he fought in actual battle for American freedom, as well as in the battles of law and legislature.

He was born on his father's farm near Dover in 1728. Most of his education came from his parents. Rodney began his public career as sheriff of Kent County. Although he had no formal schooling, he served in various court jobs and as a justice of peace. He became a judge of the supreme court for the Three Lower Counties.

Elected as a delegate to the colonial legislature in New Castle, he rose to be its speaker, a post he held until the end of colonial days. During nearly all the important meetings among the colonies leading up to the Revolution, Rodney was a chosen representative of his people.

He took an active part in the Stamp Act Congress in New York in 1765 which made the historic declaration against taxation without representation. Rodney was a writer of protests the colonies made to the King of England against the hated Townshend Act.

But he also raised his voice in the colonial meetings to demand that Delaware, which was still considered part of the Pennsylvania colony, should be given "an equal vote with any other province or government on this continent."

When the English Parliament passed a bill to close the port of Boston in 1774, as punishment for the Boston Tea Party, Rodney took it on his own to call the Delaware assembly into a special session. By law, only the royal governor had the right to do that. Rodney, however, acted on his own authority as speaker of the assembly.

The delegates appointed him and two others to attend the First Continental Congress. He was returned to the Second Continental Congress the next year. Meanwhile, he became a brigadier general of Delaware's patriot militia.

Rodney led Delaware's first direct act toward independent statehood in June 1776, by presiding over the session of the assembly at New Castle that passed a resolution declaring England no longer held power of government over the Three Counties.

During the summer of 1776, he left the debates of the Congress in Philadelphia to help put down a threatened armed uprising of British Loyalists in lower Delaware. While he was away, the voting on the Declaration of Independence neared its climax in Philadelphia.

All the colonies were not yet ready to proclaim their freedom. Delaware's vote was badly needed. But the two other delegates from the colony were divided, one of them in favor of an immediate vote for independence and one against. A messenger was sent to bring Rodney back to Philadelphia.

Rodney was then a man well past middle age. He was in poor health, exhausted from his labors of state and his military campaign to put down the Loyalists. When the messenger reached him, Rodney was in need of rest and sleep, far from fit to face a rough journey to Philadelphia on horseback.

But he began it at once. He splashed his way through shallow creeks, heavy brush, the woods and the dark of night. Swapping horses when they became too tired, he drove himself on. There were hills to climb, and at one point, Rodney and his mount fell through a plank bridge that sank beneath them. He was in physical pain, but he let nothing stop him.

The Congress in Philadelphia had begun voting and everything depended on his vote. He made it just in time. Weary and bedraggled, he burst into the council hall, breathless, his face haggard, as he rushed to the floor and gave Delaware's deciding vote for American independence.

Still with hardly any time to rest, he returned to New Castle and several weeks later took charge of the last session of the colonial assembly there. The assembly had been called to fix a date for a convention to write a constitution of statehood. Delegates were to be chosen to form Delaware's government as a state.

But Rodney had made political enemies. Despite all he had done to serve his people, there were those who thought he was too much a radical in his bold support of the cause of immediate independence. The conservatives defeated him as a delegate to the state constitutional convention.

When the new state constitution went into effect, he also failed to win election to the first state legislature. And the conservatives managed to keep him from being chosen to return to Congress that autumn as Delaware's representative.

It was a crushing blow to a man who, perhaps as much as any other, had helped Delaware become a state. But the ingratitude on the part of the voters did not dim his patriotic zeal. He turned from the halls of politics to military affairs and was named head of a branch of the Council of Safety.

At a time when the American cause reached its lowest hope of victory, Rodney's personal spirit led men to enlist in the army. He gave everything within him to recruiting needed troops and sending them forward to join the main forces.

In January 1777, after the bitter winter when all seemed nearly lost and Washington had taken up quarters at Morristown, New Jersey, Rodney was put in command of the post at Trenton. When the British invaded the state, he was leader of the forces that harassed the enemy outposts.

Delaware commissioned him general of its militia and in the spring Rodney's political fortunes began to rise again. The state legislature selected him a judge of the admiralty and then chose him as a member of the Continental Congress. The following year, Rodney was made president of the state for a term of three years.

He served as Delaware's chief executive throughout the war, fulfilling the tasks of furnishing the state's quota of Continental troops, arming and clothing them, and raising provisions and money. At war's end, he resigned because of serious illness.

In the fall of 1783, he was elected once more to office, as a member of the upper house of the legislature. His fellow lawmakers honored him by making him speaker, but Rodney died before the year's sessions ended.

Four years later, Delaware earned the proud name of "The First State" when it ratified the new Constitution of the United States. Delaware's chief executive became a governor instead of a president and the Three Counties at last had won permanent self-rule.

Rodney was buried at his farm, Poplar Grove. More than a century after his death, his last remains were moved to an honored final resting place in the churchyard of Christ Episcopal Church in Dover.

PENNSYLVANIA

Motto: Virtue, Liberty and Independence
Flower: Mountain Laurel   Bird: Ruffed Grouse
Tree: Eastern Hemlock
Admitted to the Union: 1787

☆

Fur trade with the Indians first brought explorers into the Delaware River area of what became Pennsylvania. Soon the English, Dutch and Swedes were disputing rights to the region. In 1681, England's King Charles II granted almost all of what is now Pennsylvania to William Penn, in payment of a royal debt owed to Penn's father.

Quaker Penn made treaties with the Indians and set up a government which guaranteed the colonists complete religious freedom and some rights of self-rule through an assembly. However, even in those days, the settlers wanted more power to govern themselves. After much conflict over control of the province, Penn formed a new constitution which increased the power of the assembly.

In the years that led to the Revolution, Philadelphia became the finest city in the nation. The spirit of rebellion was fed by the independence of rugged settlers of the frontier areas. Many Pennsylvanians became important leaders of the Revolutionary movement. Committees of Safety were formed and the provincial government gradually was taken over by groups favoring the patriot cause.

Philadelphia was the scene of the First and Second Continental Congresses, the signing of the Declaration of Independence and the framing of the Federal Constitution in 1787. But it was in the liberty year of 1776 that a new liberal

14

state government, the Commonwealth of Pennsylvania, was adopted. In 1790, a new state constitution reaffirmed the principles of freedom and equality for all men.

THOMAS MIFFLIN
(1744–1800)

Thomas Mifflin, a rich man's son who became a fiery rebel patriot, was called by John Adams the "animating soul" of the Revolution. He turned his back on his conservative family upbringing to become soldier, orator, statesman. From the start of independence, through all the troubled years of its early government, Mifflin helped lead Pennsylvania to statehood.

His father was a wealthy merchant, descended from the earliest settlers of the area, and young Thomas was educated at a Quaker school. He graduated from college when he was sixteen, worked in a countinghouse to prepare for the business career his family expected him to follow, and set up a partnership with a brother. It was almost immediately successful and prosperous.

But Thomas was an eloquent speaker in the cause of freedom and his ambition soon led him away from business and into politics. He was still in his twenties when he was first elected to the provincial assembly, where he served for four years. Soon recognized as a champion of colonial rights, he helped arouse sentiment for a congress of the colonies.

He became one of the youngest and most radical members of the First Continental Congress, helped to draft some of its bills, and used his luxuriously furnished home as a rendezvous for the delegates. Elected to the Second Continental Congress, he began to turn his attention to recruiting and training troops. When news of the Battle of Lexington reached Philadelphia, he took to the platform at a town meeting to whip up the fighting spirit of the crowd.

"Let us not be bold in declarations and afterwards cold in

15

action," he warned. "Let not the patriotic feeling of today be forgotten tomorrow, nor have it said of Philadelphia that she passed noble resolutions, slept upon them, and afterwards forgot them."

A man of action as well as of words, Mifflin served courageously in several early battles of the Revolution. He became General Washington's trusted friend and aide-de-camp. As Quartermaster General of the Continental Army, he was in charge of supplying the ragged and ill-organized Revolutionary troops.

In the darkest days of the war, when defeat seemed near, Washington sent Mifflin to make personal appeals to the people of Pennsylvania to support the cause. Day and night, often without sleep, he roused the crowds that gathered in front of churches, on courthouse steps, and in forest clearings to hear him.

The Quakers, who abhorred war, read Mifflin out of meeting for his military activities. Many of his conservative friends turned against him and considered him a radical. Frequently he was outspoken when it cost him dearly to voice his feelings.

A man impatient for victory, he was accused of taking part in a plot to overthrow Washington as Commander in Chief because he felt that Washington wasn't acting swiftly enough. In those days of confusion and scant means to supply an army, Mifflin also was threatened with court-martial for failing to get equipment to the men during the ordeal at Valley Forge.

He tried to do too much and his health started to fail. Generous to a fault and extravagant in his living, he became careless about personal finances and began to go heavily into debt. Torn by many conflicts, he often was as impulsive as he was prudent, sometimes prideful and vain, and in turn reckless or calm. A handsome man of medium height and athletic build who always dressed in the best fashion of the times, Mifflin also was a person of refinement, agreeable manners and a warmly friendly temperament.

He rose to be a general and member of the Board of War, but finally resigned from the army. Even after his resignation, Congress called upon him to help with military planning.

Turning again to politics, he served in the state assembly and helped to reframe Pennsylvania's constitution, as well as to set up financial policies.

Elected a member of the Federal Congress once more, he became its president in 1783 and acted in that position to guide the fate of the young nation during the closing events of the Revolution. As president, it was Mifflin who received the resignation of Washington as Commander in Chief. They had become friends again, after their earlier disagreement.

Mifflin was a member of the assembly of the state which met in 1785, and he was elected its speaker. While helping to forge statehood for Pennsylvania, he also helped form the United States Constitution. His name was affixed to that document as a member of the Constitutional Convention of 1787.

The next year, Mifflin was elected to the Supreme Executive Council of Pennsylvania and served for two years as head of state. He was chairman of the state's constitutional convention. But in his personal life, there was again sadness. During that year of 1790, the charming Quaker girl he had married, his wife Sarah, died.

Bowed by his own tragedy, Mifflin also faced a political struggle with those who were against the new constitution. He held together his political forces, overwhelmingly defeated his opponents and became Pennsylvania's first state governor.

Mifflin skillfully managed the heated debates that arose and piloted the constitution through to adoption. But after he became governor, he faced all the fresh troubles that came to perplex the new state. Through those formative years, he continued to serve, remaining governor to the end of the maximum period of three terms he was allowed to hold the office.

He established the procedure of the new executive office, worked out disputes between the state and the equally new Federal Government, saw through many of the laws that set up systems of roads and waterways, judicial and penal institutions, and helped put down two direct armed threats.

One was the Whisky Rebellion, an armed uprising in Pennsylvania's western counties against excise taxes, the defeat of which proved the government's power to enforce its

17

laws. The other was the brief insurrection led by traveling auctioneer John Fries, who had stirred a band of farmers into open revolt against property taxes.

During all his time in office, Mifflin was beset by the money troubles of the postwar years, by the great upheaval caused by the westward movement of settlers, and by the generally disturbed conditions of the times.

He anxiously wanted to retire to private life when his years as governor were over, but the people, unwilling to give up his services entirely, re-elected him a member of the legislature. He took his seat, but died during a session of the house in Lancaster in January 1800.

Mifflin, who had sacrificed his health and fortune to his career, was buried by the state, which erected a monument to the memory of its pioneer governor, soldier and state builder.

NEW JERSEY

Motto: Liberty and Prosperity

Flower: Purple Violet   Bird: Eastern Goldfinch

Tree: Red Oak

Admitted to the Union: 1787

☆

Henry Hudson sailed into Newark Bay in 1609 to give the Dutch first claim to what later became New Jersey. Dutch settlements were established and then Swedish communities. When the English took over, they encouraged settlement by providing a liberal charter that allowed for an elected assembly.

During the late 1600's there was much confusion over various land grants. The first democratic constitution was framed in 1681. Under royal rule, the governor of New York held authority over New Jersey until 1738.

The royal governors often gave in to the colonial assembly in granting desired laws and privileges because the assembly controlled the public funds. There was strong British sympathy in parts of Jersey in the years that led to the Revolution, but the desire for free government grew with the spirit of the patriot cause.

In June 1776, the provincial congress adopted a constitution and declared New Jersey a state. But in the war years, it sometimes was a state only in name as it became one of the major battlegrounds of the Revolution.

At the Federal Constitutional Convention in 1787, the delegates from New Jersey championed the cause of the smaller states and helped to carry the plan that gave each state equal representation in the Senate. New Jersey itself was the third state to ratify the Constitution.

19

WILLIAM LIVINGSTON
(1713–1790)

Throughout most of his life, William Livingston longed for the peace and quiet of the country. His ambition was to enjoy the calm existence of a gentleman farmer. He wanted to devote himself to gardening, to writing poetry and essays, and to his library and the gracious living his wealth could provide.

Instead, he spent a lifetime in public office, helping to create and to hold together an infant state, to lead it through the war years in which his own life and personal safety were constantly threatened, and to bring it into the nation of states he helped guide into being.

As most lives are measured, Livingston had two full careers. He retired at the age of fifty, believing that his life as a political leader was ended. It really had just begun and lasted nearly another two decades, during which New Jersey repeatedly named him its governor by almost unanimous vote, and refused to let him retire again.

Born a New Yorker, he spent his early childhood in Albany, where he was raised in princely style. When he was fourteen, he lived for a year with a missionary among the friendly Mohawk Indians. His family thought the experience would be valuable if he decided to enter the fur trade or to buy up lands along the frontier.

Sent to Yale in the hope that he would study to become a merchant like his three successful older brothers, he soon developed an interest in law. Livingston avoided his brothers' countinghouses and entered the law offices of James Alexander, who had battled in the courts for freedom of the press.

He won recognition in New York as a leader of those who supported the rights of the common man. Although never much of a public speaker, his clever poems and articles in a newspaper started by his friends poked fun at the aristocrats who were against democracy, and gained him a wide following. He spoke up for home rule and against letting the British Parliament interfere in affairs of the provinces.

Elected to New York's provincial legislature, Livingston served three terms. But in the election of 1769 he was overwhelmingly defeated. He quit politics, convinced that his public career was over.

Livingston bought an estate near Elizabethtown, New Jersey. He laid out the grounds, planted a large orchard and built a mansion that became known as Liberty Hall. There he hoped to take his life of ease. He had come past middle age and felt it was time to retire.

But he also felt too strongly about the American cause to still his pen. Soon he was writing broadsides to arouse the people. He became a member of a county Committee of Correspondence and quickly rose to leadership greater than he previously had held in his native New York.

As one of New Jersey's delegates to the First and Second Continental Congresses, Livingston helped to draft many of the important political documents of those times. In the spring of 1776 he took command of the New Jersey troops of Revolution, a responsibility he didn't want, but one that he carried out with great ability. Livingston served in command until the legislature, under the new constitution, elected him first governor of the state.

For fourteen years he bore the responsibilities of the governorship, personally holding the state government together during the severe hardships of the war and the troubled days of reconstruction. As wartime governor he kept aflame the spirit of resistance in a people who often lost confidence in their barefoot and ragged army, and kept them firm against the panic of near defeat.

He headed a defenseless legislature that wandered from Princeton to Burlington and from Pitt's Town to Haddonfield, trying to find a safe place to hold its meetings. For a time, the legislature dissolved and there remained almost nothing of the struggling new state government, except for the leadership of Livingston himself.

Livingston calmed the people alarmed by the British invasion, helped promote laws to end traffic with the enemy, to settle problems of plunder, of refugees, of conflicting land and property claims. When General Washington called on him to raise "men, not money," Livingston led his legislature into voting stricter laws of military service. But he did so with a patience that understood that the people had just freed themselves from one government which had been charged with oppression and were in no mood for iron-handed rule by the new state.

The British put a price on Livingston's head, and made many attempts to destroy his property, to burn down his home and to capture or kill him. One time his house was surrounded at night by an enemy party that waited until dawn to attack. Livingston escaped being taken prisoner by fleeing to a neighboring village before the sun was up.

Through all the years of trouble, he continued to be chosen governor at each election, often unanimously. When peace finally approached, he was nearing his sixties, an old man whose greatest desire had always been for quiet country life. He returned to Elizabethtown with great joy at being able to give up his wandering and to be with his wife and children, to have time to raise flowers and vegetables "which, with the additional pleasure resulting from my library, I really prefer to all the splendor of the world."

Still, his retirement wasn't to be. New Jersey and the new nation of which it was part had need of William Livingston. He wanted to quit the governorship, but the people would not let him.

Peace had lifted some of the problems of the separate states, but those of the new Federal Government were increased. There was no longer any bond of common danger against the enemy and the Confederation had lost public respect. It was hard to get enough Representatives in Congress for it to act at all. Livingston said that unless something was done quickly, he doubted that "the liberty for which we have so strenuously contended" would survive.

By his own efforts, he led New Jersey to approve a call for revising the Articles of Confederation. He influenced his state to form and adopt a constitution. Appointed a delegate to the federal convention, he was chairman of a committee that drafted parts of the United States Constitution. As one of the few who also had been in Congress at the time of the Declaration of Independence, Livingston had great influence.

He guided the New Jersey delegates, signed the Constitution, returned to Elizabethtown and was immediately re-elected governor. Through his efforts, on December 18, 1787, New Jersey became the third of the states to ratify. His state's approval was unanimous.

"We are now arrived to that auspicious period which I confess I have so often wished that it might please Heaven to protract my life to see," he told the legislature. "Thanks to God that I have lived to see it."

The people again refused to let him retire, although he took a less active part in national affairs. Livingston did find time at last to cultivate his gardens, amused himself reading and writing and using the tools of a home workshop where he built birdhouses he proudly put up around the grounds.

At each fall election for governor, he received the grateful tribute of respect and affection the people gave their "grand old man." There was no political intrigue that could remove him from the office he held through the remainder of his life.

On a July Sunday in 1790, while resting at his beloved Elizabethtown estate, he died at the age of seventy-seven. Through war and peace, against his personal desire to escape public life, William Livingston had led New Jersey from the birth of independence to statehood.

GEORGIA

Motto: Wisdom, Justice, Moderation

Flower: Cherokee Rose   Bird: Brown Thrasher

Tree: Live Oak

Admitted to the Union: 1788

☆

Georgia, the last of the English colonies established in America, took its name from King George II.

The British were anxious to create a colony that would stand in the way of the Spaniards in Florida and keep them from invading South Carolina. At the same time, a group of wealthy men in England hoped to provide a place in the New World for worthy people who were poor and had fallen into debt. Georgia became the project of their charity and began as a carefully planned colony of chosen settlers.

The settlers of 1733 were personally led to what later became Savannah by James Oglethorpe, a British general and longtime member of Parliament, under a charter granted to the trustees. Georgia at first made such slow progress and caused so much trouble that the trustees were glad to turn it back to the Crown in 1753 when their charter expired.

It then became a royal colony, with the British paying nearly all the colonial expenses until the period just before the Revolution. At the outbreak of war, Georgia was the weakest and least populated of the thirteen colonies. But it was the fourth to ratify the Constitution and the first of the Southern states to do so.

The hardest part of its struggle for statehood was in arousing the people to break with British rule. In Georgia, the Revolution amounted almost to a civil war, with Loyalist and Revolutionary parties nearly equal.

ARCHIBALD BULLOCH

(1730–1777)

Archibald Bulloch was born in South Carolina three years before Georgia became an English settlement. It still was not a royal colony when he moved there with his family as a young man of twenty.

The Bullochs settled in a home near the Savannah River and Archibald's father, who had been a clergyman in Scotland, became a planter. Archibald worked on the plantation while he finished his studies for a law career.

He began to practice law in Savannah, married a judge's daughter, and soon became prominent in politics. By then, Savannah was starting to grow into a lively little port city, although the rest of the colony still was mostly frontier settlements.

Under the royal governor, James Wright, Georgia had begun to prosper. Wright believed that the soil of the swamps and lowlands along the coasts and rivers could grow rice. His theory proved true and a number of rice plantations flourished. Most of the big landowners approved the royal government and many settlers felt strong ties with Britain. They had no real complaint against Wright, even if some did sympathize with the other colonies.

Everywhere there was talk of British oppression in the rest of the colonies, talk of free government, and Bulloch was a young idealist who was first a friend and then a leader of the liberals. Never a man to go into anything halfheartedly, he became convinced that Georgia should be delivered from kingly domain and devoted all his energy to arousing others to support the cause of freedom.

When the English Parliament extended the Stamp Tax to include America, Bulloch led Georgia's stand against it. He was among those who demanded that Governor Wright summon the Georgia royal assembly so the members could vote on the tax. This the governor refused to do.

In April 1772, Bulloch was chosen speaker of the Georgia assembly. To keep him from taking charge, the governor dissolved the assembly immediately after Bulloch was elected. Bulloch then urged the people to refuse food and lodging for British troops stationed in Savannah, which they did until they were forced to give in because of a threatened Indian attack against the colony.

He boldly signed his name to the first call, in June 1774, for an independent assembly of patriots in Savannah. The turnout was disappointing because there were many who sided with the British or who were content to let things go along as they were. Within months, however, as the flame of revolution grew, a convention of patriot delegates from throughout Georgia did meet.

The delegates met at the same time as the scheduled session of the royal assembly and Bulloch was elected president of that first provincial congress. He also was named a Georgia delegate to the Continental Congress.

Royal Governor Wright made threats and issued stern proclamations. Bulloch and patriot rebels ignored them. Some of the royalists began to flee to safety. The patriots seized the city's powder magazine to arm themselves and captured a powder ship that lay in the mouth of the river.

Wright again tried to call the royal assembly into session. Instead, the provincial convention met again on its own. An executive council was chosen and Bulloch was made its head. Under his leadership, Georgia actually became an independent state, administering its own affairs in defiance of the royal government. Governor Wright was captured and made a prisoner in his own home, but managed to escape to one of the British sloops of war anchored near Savannah.

However, Bulloch still had to contend with a divided homeland. Many Georgians continued to oppose the new provincial congress. It required all his political skill as well as personal courage to keep the self-declared state functioning.

But Bulloch's courage wasn't limited to affairs of state. He

26

took to the battlefield himself, as leader of a party of militia and Creek Indians that destroyed the British and Tory base on Tybee Island.

In February 1777 the "whole executive power of government" was put into his hands as Georgia's president and commander in chief. The same month, the provincial government framed its state constitution. But near the end of February, Bulloch was stricken ill and died at his Savannah home.

He was forty-seven years old and had given nearly half those years to the making of a state. When he died, the war was far from decided and independence was in grave doubt of success, but he had lived long enough to see Georgia move toward the formal statehood he helped to create.

The British seized Savannah in 1778 and revived the royal government. They recaptured other important parts of the colony and held control for four years, until the tide of victory began to turn. Civil affairs fell into confusion and it wasn't until the early 1780's that the new state really began to operate on its own again.

When the delegates from all the colonies met in the Constitutional Convention of 1787, Georgia's representatives took a firm stand for strong federal government. Still one of the smallest states in population, Georgia voted with the larger ones, partly because it claimed all the territory westward to the Mississippi and hoped to become large itself.

Georgia's delegates gave their support to measures designed to strengthen national government along the lines Archibald Bulloch had fought for in the years of his life. In January 1788 Georgia became the fourth state to ratify the Federal Constitution, and was one of only three of the original states that did so by unanimous vote.

CONNECTICUT

Motto: He Who Transplanted Still Sustains

Flower: Mountain Laurel   Bird: American Robin

Tree: White Oak

Admitted to the Union: 1788

☆

Long before many of the other colonies, Connecticut had a written constitution and a government by elected representatives. Although the area was discovered by the Dutch in 1614, the first permanent settlers were English colonists from Massachusetts.

Its long history of representative government began with Thomas Hooker. He was one of the liberty-loving Puritan ministers who had come to Boston by way of Holland, where he had fled to escape arrest for his preaching. Chosen pastor of a church at Cambridge, he found himself in conflict with Massachusetts authorities over his democratic views. In the spring of 1636, he led a party of about a hundred members of his congregation, with their goods and cattle, westward across the wilderness to settle near what became Hartford.

Two years later, the Reverend Hooker preached a great sermon setting forth the principles which became the basis of the commonwealth formed by leaders of three Connecticut River towns. He declared that "the foundation of authority is laid in the free consent of the people," and that they should be allowed to choose their public magistrates and have the privilege of election. Hooker ended his sermon with the ringing words, "As God has given us liberty, let us take it."

Called the Fundamental Orders, these principles were

drawn up to be submitted to a mass meeting of the people, which adopted them. The right to vote was given to all free men. Executive and judicial powers were vested in the governor and his six assistants, these officers to be elected annually in a general assembly. The plan provided for a legislature of deputies from the various towns.

Meanwhile, the area around New Haven was settled by another group, which established its own government along less liberal lines. Both colonies lived in complete independence of England, of Massachusetts, and of one another. They established their own courts and made their own laws.

The Hartford colony elected John Winthrop its governor in 1657 and he visited England and obtained from King Charles II the Charter of Connecticut. This not only confirmed all the liberties the river towns had enjoyed, but also set boundaries which brought the New Haven colony under the same jurisdiction. Under its provisions, Connecticut flourished for more than a century and a half.

When King James II decided to unite all New England under the government of Massachusetts, Connecticut was commanded to surrender its charter. The King's agent, Sir Edmund Andros, and his troops appeared before the general assembly in Hartford and demanded that the charter be handed over to him in the King's name.

According to legend, the document was brought forth and laid on the table. But suddenly all the lights were extinguished. When the candles were relighted, the charter mysteriously had disappeared. The tradition is that it was hidden from the British in the heart of a great oak tree in Hartford, which afterwards became known as the Charter Oak.

Two years later, James II abdicated and the danger to Connecticut's free government ended. But even when it became an independent state, after the Revolution, Connecticut did not adopt a new constitution. For some forty years after signing the Declaration of Independence, it continued under the Charter of 1662. It wasn't until 1818 that a new state constitution finally was adopted.

JONATHAN TRUMBULL

(*1710–1785*)

The son of a country storekeeper, who studied to become a minister and became instead a businessman and then a lawyer, Jonathan Trumbull served Connecticut in public office for fifty-one years.

Elected twenty-three times to the legislature and fifteen times as governor, he led his state from Crown colony through revolution to independence. He was the only royal colonial governor to continue in office after independence was declared.

Trumbull's ancestors came from England to Massachusetts and then to the Hartford colony. His father moved to the little town of Lebanon and started business there as a merchant and farmer about ten years before Jonathan was born.

When Jonathan was only thirteen, he entered Harvard College. He dedicated himself to becoming a minister, was licensed to preach and was called to a church at Colchester. Before he could take the pulpit there, his older brother was lost at sea.

In the sinking that took his brother's life, a cargo ship and all the goods aboard that belonged to Jonathan's father were lost. By then, his father was an aged man and there was nobody else to settle up the accounts and carry on the family business. At his father's pleading, Jonathan reluctantly gave up the ministry to take charge of the store.

He soon was a far more successful merchant than his father and brother had been. Young Jonathan set up trade connections to import his goods directly from London, rather than dealing through Boston or New York as most other merchants did. He became one of the outstanding figures of Connecticut commerce in the 1760's.

During the years he was in business, he also was studying law. Having won the respect and confidence of his neighbors, he was first elected to the general assembly of the royal colony in 1733.

When he took his seat as a lawmaker, Jonathan was only twenty-three years old. He still hadn't reached his thirtieth birthday when he was made speaker for the first time. The following year he was chosen a member of the governing council and in 1766 became lieutenant governor of the colony and chief judge of the superior court.

Although his position made him an officer of the Crown, Jonathan identified himself from the beginning with the patriot cause. He stood firmly against the right claimed by the British Parliament to tax the colonies as it pleased. When called upon by the British to take the oath required of every official to support the Stamp Act, Jonathan flatly refused.

When Governor William Pitkin died in 1769, the assembly named Jonathan Trumbull to the governorship, a position he held under one Connecticut government or another for the rest of his life, until he decided himself at the age of seventy-four that he was too old to go on with it and retired. During those momentous years of resistance, rebellion and independence, he guided Connecticut into being as a state.

Physically, he was an active man whose many duties gave him good reason to seem in a hurry. He was tall, handsomely figured, with prominent facial features and alert dark eyes. Jonathan had little interest in the lighter things of life or in what he considered trivial. Perhaps his stern sense of duty was part of his Puritan heritage.

He enjoyed reading Hebrew, Greek and Latin and corresponded widely with leaders abroad as well as with those of the Revolution, including his friend General Washington, to whom he frequently gave advice.

It was his hope at first, as it was with many other statesmen of those times, that the troubles between the colonies and Great Britain could be settled "by gentle methods rather than by power and force." But as the crisis deepened in the early months of 1775, he called a special session of the assembly to prepare the colony for the "last extremity."

When the battles at Lexington and Concord plunged America into full-scale fighting, Trumbull called the assembly into meeting again and solemnly told the session that the only alternative to war was "subjugation and slavery."

In theory, Connecticut was still a royal colony and he was a royal governor, but Trumbull soon led the legislature to pass laws that made it a crime to be loyal to the empire either in word or deed. Reference to the royal government was removed from the oaths of loyalty and the new oaths demanded allegiance only to the "colony and government . . . as established by charter."

Connecticut legally began to assume the powers of independence in June 1776 when an extraordinary meeting of the assembly authorized its delegates to Congress "to declare the United American Colonies Free and Independent States." By October, official records referred to "the State of Connecticut in New England in America."

When the Declaration of Independence was approved, Connecticut's people were freed from "all allegiance to the British Crown" and all political connections with Britain were declared at an end.

However, the assembly was careful to state that the form of government established by the old royal charter would otherwise continue unchanged, since most of the existing laws did not prevent Connecticut's "absolute independence."

Under Trumbull's leadership, Connecticut freely gave of men and wealth during the whole Revolution. Its soldiers were on battle lines from Quebec to the Carolinas. Connecticut was known as the "provision state" where "Brother Jonathan" always could be depended upon for supplies that the struggling armies of the Republic needed.

His belief in the need for a strong central government brought him into new political conflicts in 1783 and he decided to retire. Then an old man, just passing his seventy-third birthday, he told the assembly the following summer that he would not be a candidate for re-election.

Reflecting on his "advanced state of life, a life worn out almost in the constant cares of office," he said, "I think it my duty to retire from the busy concerns of public affairs."

But in his moving retirement address, he made a plea for a federal union that would be stronger both politically and financially than the existing government. While he did not live to see his state ratify the Constitution, his urgent words helped to arouse sentiment in favor of that final act of statehood that came in 1788, three years after Jonathan Trumbull died.

MASSACHUSETTS

Motto: By the Sword We Seek Peace, but Peace Only Under Liberty

Flower: Trailing Arbutus

Bird: Chickadee

Tree: American Elm

Admitted to the Union: 1788

☆

When the Pilgrims, seeking religious freedom, set sail for North America in 1620 and established their colony at Plymouth, they brought the start of democratic government to Massachusetts. Their Mayflower Compact was an agreement that bound all to conform to the will of the majority.

But the real foundation of the commonwealth came when John Winthrop and a group of Puritans arrived at Salem in 1630 bearing with them a charter to establish a self-contained English colony governed by its own members.

Power was put in the hands of the governor and in a court of assistants and freemen, who were first the stockholders of the Massachusetts Bay Company, but who later included all respectable landowners. They began to send representatives to attend the meetings that grew into a legislative assembly.

The Massachusetts Bay Colony worked out its problems without much interference from across the sea until the charter was taken away in 1684 and the colony became the absolute property of the King to govern as he saw fit. All the territory of New England soon was added to New York and New Jersey and Sir Edmund Andros, already governor of the two southern colonies, was made governor of all.

Andros swept away free government and ruled as a despot. But when James II was overthrown as England's king, the people of Massachusetts revolted against Andros. An uprising of armed men in Boston forced his surrender and restored the rights of the commonwealth.

Massachusetts again became a separate royal colony, under a governor appointed by the Crown. Two legislative houses were permitted. But soon there was new resentment over the growing restrictions against the will of the people to govern themselves. Finally, there came a series of British acts which led to open defiance and the Revolution.

In 1775, after the fight at Concord, the revolutionary provincial congress declared that the royal governor no longer was their executive and ordered an election of the legislature under the old charter. The house adopted the old charter, without a governor, and put executive power in a council. But many felt that the provincial congress did not properly represent the people and a struggle for true constitutional government began.

THEOPHILUS PARSONS
(1750–1813)

The whole plan for a strong government of united American states hung in the balance in Massachusetts in the winter of 1788. The spring before, delegates from the states had met in Philadelphia and finally had worked out a federal constitution. When it came before the state convention in Massachusetts, however, there was grave doubt that it would be accepted.

If Massachusetts refused to ratify, then New York, Virginia and other states also might refuse. Some of the states that had already approved might try to change their minds.

George Washington was worried. "What will be the fate of the Constitution in this state it is impossible to tell," he wrote. And James Madison declared, "I am in doubt whether they will approve the Constitution."

Many of the delegates who assembled in Boston from the various towns of the state were hostile to the Constitution because they were afraid of greater taxes or of losing liberties newly won in the Revolution. Samuel Adams was against it. So was John Hancock. Both men had enormous influence. Their pride and political power were in the state and they were heartily opposed to any federal government that might lessen the sovereignty of Massachusetts.

As the delegates began their debates, John Hancock stayed away from the convention, pleading illness, but really waiting things out to see which way the tide of opinion might turn.

The man who was the guiding spirit of the political struggle to bring Massachusetts into the Union was Theophilus Parsons. Then still in his thirties, he was a brilliant young lawyer who already had helped give his state its own constitution.

Born in 1750, the son of the parish minister at Byfield, Parsons became perhaps the most eminent lawyer and jurist in all New England during the years in which he lived. Although he never held any really important political office and shunned public attention and personal fame, his mind and his pen influenced the entire concept of American government.

Even as a schoolboy, it was said that Parsons worked harder and played harder than any of his companions. Sent to Harvard with the help of contributions from members of his father's church congregation, he graduated when he was nineteen and took a job teaching school at what was then Falmouth, now Portland, Maine. While he was teaching he also studied law, and finally began a promising practice in Falmouth.

His prospects for success as a small-town lawyer came to a sudden end in 1775 when British ships of war attacked the city. Falmouth was burned and almost entirely destroyed. Crushed by the calamity, Parsons returned to his home in Byfield. It seemed to him that everything had been lost, but the tragedy was one of the most fortunate things that happened to him.

When he reached his father's house, he found Judge Edmund Trowbridge staying there. Trowbridge had fled from his own home in Cambridge because of his suspected sympathy with the British. In young Parsons, the judge discovered a devoted law student.

Trowbridge owned what was then the best law library in the colony. He sent for all his books, so Parsons could study them. From the books Parsons gained a greater knowledge of both English and colonial laws than was available to most other lawyers.

While others were fighting for independence, Parsons became concerned about what kind of permanent government would follow victory. By the time the Declaration of Independence was signed, he was practicing law in Newburyport. The opinions he had begun to form were treated with respect by men far older and politically more powerful.

A group of Berkshire County farmers, led by the Reverend Thomas Allen, petitioned the state legislature for a constitution "to provide for posterity against the wanton exercise of power." Others demanded a convention to form a better state government. Early in 1778, a state constitution was agreed upon by the legislature and offered to the people.

When Parsons and his friends read it, they were alarmed by the weaknesses they found. Parsons wrote what has since become a historic pamphlet, known as "The Essex Result." It was a detailed study of the main principles of republican government and became the plan largely followed by John Adams and others in drafting the Massachusetts constitution of 1780.

Parsons called for a bill of rights, said that the legislative, judicial and executive powers should be lodged in different hands with a system of checks and balances, and outlined the need for compromises to serve the greatest good of individuals as well as the people as a whole.

The immediate effect of the widely circulated pamphlet was felt in town meetings throughout the state that voted against the proposed poor state constitution. But beyond that, it had an influence on the structure of constitutions in other states and on the thinking that went into making the Constitution of the United States.

Parsons was named to a committee to draft a better state constitution for Massachusetts. It was approved, after revisions, with Parsons taking a leading part in the debates as a convention delegate. After that, he had very little active interest in politics for the next five or six years. He was busy as a lawyer and in providing for his growing family.

A tall, heavily built, restless man, with penetrating dark eyes, he cared nothing about his personal appearance. His wife once said she had to follow him about to make sure he was dressed well enough to be seen. When he was in his early thirties, he started to turn bald and afterward wore a wig that, as often as not, was on crookedly.

In his spare time he relaxed with a book of Greek, by working out problems in algebra, or by writing papers on astronomy. Sometimes he shut himself in a workshop where he made toys for his children and furniture for his home.

The last thing he seemed to want was to become a political leader, especially not one who might be called upon to make speeches. But in 1787, Parsons became a member of the state legislature, because he felt his services once again were needed. The storm had begun to grow over approval of the Federal Constitution.

He went as a delegate to the convention that gathered the next year at Boston's old Meeting House in Long Lane. Soon he was leader of the debates on the floor, voicing his appeals for Massachusetts to ratify the document that would create the United States. Behind the scenes, he worked even harder to win John Hancock's support.

After staying away for twenty-two days, Hancock finally appeared and took his place as president of the convention. Parsons arose and moved for a vote to approve the Constitution. Hancock announced that he had a plan of compromise. He dramatically called for an adjournment until that afternoon.

There were whispers that a deal had been made, that Hancock realized there was some chance the Constitution might win in Massachusetts despite his opposition, and that he had agreed to throw his support to those in favor of it in exchange for future political rewards.

That afternoon, Hancock submitted proposed amendments to the Constitution, not as conditions demanded before Massachusetts would ratify it, but as recommendations that should be considered by the first Congress. The proposals saved the Constitution and were the basis of the Bill of Rights.

Massachusetts thus became first to suggest and adopt a practical method of securing both ratification and amendment, a method soon followed by other states, especially Virginia and New York.

In Boston that day when the vote at last was taken, one hundred sixty-eight delegates still were against the Constitution. But one hundred eighty-seven were for it. By a margin of only nineteen votes, Massachusetts became one of the new United States. Throughout the city there was great rejoicing. There were parades, fireworks, dinners, speeches and demonstrations by singing, cheering crowds who shouted John Hancock's name as the hero of the hour.

But the recommendations Hancock had read, and had not even seen until just before he offered them, were written by Theophilus Parsons.

Parsons, with the advice of the others who supported the Constitution, had drawn them up and delivered them to Hancock, with the understanding that Hancock and his group would get full credit for them.

Hancock never claimed that the actual words he read were his own. If his pride was involved, so was his desire to do what seemed best for his country, the same desire that Parsons had in seeking the compromise that the Massachusetts patriots found together.

Hancock served his state as its first governor. Parsons became chief justice of the state supreme court. In that position, he wrote many of the opinions that became the body of the state's law. In the two decades in which he served his state, after that day of historic Constitutional decision, he never again took a direct part in politics.

John Adams offered to make Parsons the nation's Attorney General but he refused the honor. He died in 1813 at the age of sixty-three, after a brief illness. In his final hours, with his mind wandering over the past, Parsons seemed to imagine himself in his courtroom, and his last words were: "Brethren of the jury, the case is closed and in your hands. . . . ."

MARYLAND

Motto: Manly Deeds, Womanly Words; *and* With the Shield of Thy
Good-will Thou Hast Covered Us

Flower: Black-eyed Susan   Bird: Baltimore Oriole

Tree: White Oak

Admitted to the Union: 1788

Self-government began in Maryland almost from the time the
colony was founded. In the spring of 1633, two vessels, the
Ark and the *Dove,* brought some two hundred settlers from
England. The colony was the first to guarantee full religious
freedom and, within five years of its settlement, the colonists
sought the right to make their own laws.

The charter granted by King Charles I to Lord Baltimore
had given him the power to call an assembly only if and
when he so desired. But the colonists won a surrender of that
claim. In 1650 one of the two houses of the assembly was
made up entirely of representatives of the freemen, whose consent was needed before a bill could become law.

The Council House at St. Mary's, which was the capital of
the flourishing colony before Annapolis was chosen as the
seat of government, also heard the first demand for women's
rights in 1648. Margaret Brent, an owner of extensive prop-
erties, became a power in the colony as Lord Baltimore's
representative. She held the purse, collected the revenues, paid
the colony's employees and was, in fact if not in title, its acting executive.

Mistress Brent appeared before the general assembly, declared that the laws discriminated against women, and asked
for the right to vote. It was a daring demand to make in those

times when women were granted no voice in the affairs of government. Although she was refused, the assembly later declared that the colony's safety was "better in her hands than any man's else in the whole province."

In 1692, the Crown set up a royal government, but the ideals of democracy remained so strong among Marylanders in the years that led toward the Declaration of Independence that the people resisted almost every form of official action that would weaken their self-rule. In turn, they sometimes voted against not only the proprietor, the royal governor, Parliament and King, but also against invasion of their rights by the Continental Congress.

THOMAS JOHNSON
(*1732–1819*)

Thomas Johnson was a reluctant rebel. He was a cautious, conservative man who didn't want to fight with anybody, certainly not the British government. But the times in which he lived shaped him to leadership.

One of his English ancestors was knighted by Charles II and others held posts of high honor, but what wealth the family had was lost by his grandfather, who migrated to Maryland. By the time Thomas grew up, there was no money to give him an education, so he went to work as a clerk in the office of Thomas Jennings, Register of Property at the state capital.

There he found two loves. One was Jennings' daughter, whom he married. The other was a love for the orderly process of law. He applied himself to the study of law, was admitted to practice, and soon won attention for his brilliant legal talent. He saved his money, found an opportunity to invest in several iron furnaces, and made himself a man of substance before he was thirty.

Although he had no strong desire to enter politics, friends convinced him that Maryland needed his services and he was elected to the state assembly in 1761. From a struggling young lawyer, he had become a man of property, and he began to write to landowners in Virginia about a plan he had to make the upper reaches of the Potomac River navigable for ships of trade.

One of the Virginia landowners with whom he corresponded was George Washington of Mount Vernon. The exchange of letters helped to broaden Johnson's political thinking. Before, he had been interested only in what was happening in Maryland, but he began to realize that the common problems of all the colonies required acting together in a common cause.

Re-elected each year to the colonial assembly, he was a member of it when the Stamp Act was passed by the British Parliament. He advocated the calling of an American congress, the first such congress to be held. Johnson was named to the committee charged with drawing up the instructions for the Maryland delegates to that assembly in New York.

Being the conservative he was, he didn't put himself in opposition to the King or favor any change of government. He urged a reasonable attitude and instructed the delegates to remind the King that he shouldn't trespass on their rights as English citizens. Johnson also was chosen to help write a memorial to the King, making clear "the constitutional rights and privileges of the freemen of the province."

Maryland's royal governor, Sir Robert Eden, impatient with actions of the state assembly, dissolved it and began issuing autocratic decrees. Johnson took to the floor with a speech in which he quietly and soberly said that the colonial governor had no right to rule by decree.

Johnson made no dramatic liberty-or-death speech, such as Patrick Henry's in Virginia, but he voiced the same feelings, that taxation without representation was tyranny. "This act of power," he declared, "is founded on destruction of constitutional security."

Having gone that far, he stood by his views and explained them more fully in a published article in which he said plainly that the final source of authority in Maryland was not the governor, nor the Lord Proprietary, not even the Crown, but only the Maryland freeman. Thus, at the age of forty-two, he found himself a revolutionary. It was 1774 and the Boston Tea Party had taken place.

Johnson's logical thinking, the beliefs of his mind and heart, not the sway of emotions, had made him a rebel. But, having reached that point, he threw off reluctance and assumed the leadership demanded of him.

After a century and a half, Maryland was without any sanctioned government. The problem was how to preserve established freedoms in a world of revolutionary change. A town-wide meeting, known as the Association of the Free Men of Maryland, was called in Baltimore and it proposed another meeting of deputies to represent all the counties of the state.

That convention was held in Annapolis in June. It recognized that the situation in Maryland was repeated in the other British colonies and moved to consult with them. Johnson was chosen one of the members to arrange for the Congress of the Colonies at Philadelphia.

When he took his seat in that congress, he was named to the three most important committees—to draw up a statement of British wrongs against the Americans, to limit imports and exports of goods between the colonies and England, and to frame a petition of rights to the King.

He reported back to another Maryland convention that voted firm approval of what the Philadelphia congress had accomplished. Johnson became a member of the state Committee of Observation, which served as the acting government of Maryland during the time when there legally was no other.

Returning as a delegate to the Second Continental Congress, as all hope for peaceful settlement with Britain finally was abandoned, he was the man selected to nominate his former letter-writing friend from Mount Vernon, George Washington, as Commander in Chief of the Continental Army.

Johnson hurried to Annapolis to urge his people to assume the full functions of government and helped to draft the declaration of rights signed by the deputies. That was in August and, a short time later, he was back in the Federal Congress, taking a lively part in its debates.

Johnson was not in Philadelphia on the day the Declaration of Independence was adopted. He was too busy helping to lead his own state to independence. One day ahead of the nation, Maryland declared itself free of England. On July 3, 1776, the state's representatives asserted that, since the King of England had violated his faith toward Maryland, it no longer recognized any obligation toward his government.

The convention was still the only functioning government when Maryland declared itself a state. In an act unusual for any government in power, it then voted itself out of existence. Johnson helped frame a new constitution for the State of Maryland that was adopted in November 1776.

Meanwhile, to add to all his other duties, he had been chosen first brigadier general of the Maryland militia. Although urged to return to the Federal Congress, he went to Frederick to raise and equip recruits. Early in 1777, he led some 1,800 men from there to George Washington's headquarters in New Jersey.

Elected by the legislature as the first governor of Maryland, he accepted by letter from Washington's camp and was inaugurated in March. Re-elected unanimously the next fall, and again without opposition the following year, he served as the chief executive of the state until 1779.

As a member of the lower house of the legislature in 1780 and early in 1781, Johnson urged adoption of the Articles of Confederation, but not until he felt convinced that the other states would surrender their claims to western lands so the territory beyond the Alleghenies would be the common property of all the United States.

When peace came, he and Washington revived the plan to extend navigation of the Potomac River. They organized a company, with Washington as president and Johnson as a member of the board of directors.

Johnson served two more terms in the legislature and was a leader of the state convention of 1788 which ratified the

Constitution. Warned by Washington that if the Maryland convention adjourned without acting it would be "tantamount to rejection of the Constitution," he used all his personal influence to help bring about Maryland's favorable vote.

He served as chief judge of the General Court of Maryland and then was appointed a justice of the United States Supreme Court. As justice, Johnson wrote the first opinion in the Reports of the United States Supreme Court.

Washington appointed him in 1791 a member of the Board of Commissioners of the new federal city and Johnson and his associates wrote to its architect, Major L'Enfant, that they had decided to call it the City of Washington.

Finally, his poor health forced him to resign as a Washington city commissioner and also from the Supreme Court and to turn down President Washington's request that he become Secretary of State. Johnson spent the later years of his life in retirement near Frederick. His last public appearance was on Washington's birthday in 1800, when he delivered an oration to his friend's memory.

Before his death, at the age of eighty-seven, Thomas Johnson remarked to friends that while he had never sought political power, he was happy in the thought that he had served his country with honor and had gained the "friendship and confidence" of Washington, and that he hoped his descendants might remember his name.

SOUTH CAROLINA

Motto: While I Breathe, I Hope; *and* Prepared in Mind and Resources
Flower: Carolina Yellow Jessamine   Bird: Carolina Wren
Tree: Palmetto
Admitted to the Union: 1788

☆

Early English settlements were made in the South Carolina region in the late 1600's and the settlers had a voice in their government almost from the beginning. By 1693, representatives in the commons house won the right to propose laws. The people guarded the privilege zealously, first against the English proprietors, whose government they overthrew in 1719, and later against the Crown.

South Carolina was a prosperous colony and its chief city of Charleston became one of the most cultured in the New World, with a theatre, frequent musical entertainments and fine libraries. Many of the young men of Charleston were educated in England and took a firm hand in both business and government when they returned home.

The people, long accustomed to self-government, secured such rights that by 1760 the royal governor and his council were hardly more than figureheads. Even though there was little real oppression in the colony itself, South Carolina joined in resisting the British, and by September 1775 the royal governor had fled.

Throughout the Revolution South Carolina was in constant conflict with British troops and also Loyalists living within its borders. It was the scene of perhaps more battles than any other colony, although many were small skirmishes. Charleston itself, first under fire a month before the Declaration of

Independence, was captured and occupied by the British in 1780.

After the war, there was fresh conflict over joining the Union. Settlers in the western upcountry part of South Carolina were mostly small farmers who had moved south from Pennsylvania and Virginia. They distrusted the sophisticated people of Charleston and were even more against the idea of giving any power to a national government that would be as far away as Philadelphia.

CHARLES PINCKNEY
(1757–1824)

Charles Pinckney was the typical son of a wealthy Southern family of planters and lawyers. His father, uncle and cousins all were active in the Revolution, although they were aristocrats by birth and closely tied to England by business and family relations.

Born October 26, 1757, Charles was the son of the president of the first South Carolina provincial congress. Unlike his equally famous cousins, Thomas Pinckney and Charles Coatesworth Pinckney, who returned to England for their education, Charles completed his schooling in America. Later, he married Mary Eleanor Laurens, daughter of another famous South Carolinian, and they had one son.

Charles Pinckney was studying law at the outbreak of the Revolution, enlisted in the militia and saw service in some of the early battles. In 1779 he also served in the state house of representatives. He was captured during the siege of Charleston the following year and remained a prisoner until the war was over.

After the war, Charles Pinckney was an outspoken delegate to the national Congress, actively campaigning for a more powerful federal government. He called for a committee to be formed to consider the internal affairs of the nation and offered a series of amendments to strengthen the Articles of Confederation.

When the Federal Constitutional Convention was held in 1787, he again represented South Carolina, along with his cousin, Charles Coatesworth Pinckney. Charles Pinckney came to the convention with a plan for the Constitution which was presented to the members right after the Virginia Plan had been proposed. Many of the ideas he argued for in the historic debates over the Constitution became part of the final document.

But when he returned home to South Carolina, some members of the state legislature were so against the Constitution they didn't even want a state convention called to consider it. Pinckney took to the floor to debate its merits with those who felt it was so worthless South Carolina shouldn't bother with it at all.

The issue was sharply divided between the group from the coastal counties who were in favor of it and the upcountry people, represented by Rawlins Lowndes. Lowndes declared that the old Articles of Confederation provided for all the central government the nation needed and that he was against any "experiments" with a new constitution. He warned that if it was ever adopted the "sun of the Southern states would set, never to rise again."

Patiently and diplomatically, Pinckney answered each point that was questioned. With his knowledge as one of the planners of the Constitution, and his skill as a lawyer and statesman, he managed to lead the legislature to decide that a convention should be called to ratify or reject it.

At the convention itself, he took the lead in presenting the case for ratification. Keeping in mind the vast differences between the two areas of his own state, he pointed out that there were also great differences among the states that had already approved the Constitution, as well as among the delegates who had framed the document.

When the issue actually was put to a vote, there was less opposition than there had been during the fight in the legislature. At one point it was touch and go, when word was received in South Carolina that Virginia might withhold its approval. But Pinckney won the convention battle. On May 23, 1788, South Carolina voted one hundred forty-nine to seventy-three to ratify the Constitution of the United States.

Pinckney turned some of his family and friends against him by endorsing the Republican policies of Thomas Jefferson. But that unexpectedly won him the support of upcountry voters who helped elect him to the Senate in 1798.

Later he was named ambassador to Spain, but was not as good a diplomat as he had been a statesman and soon was recalled. He served again as governor and also in Congress. In giving so much of his time to serving in places away from home, he allowed his estate to become poorly managed. During the years before his death, he was reduced to living on a far more modest scale than he had in his lavish younger years.

He had, however, earned the rich respect and honor of the state he helped create.

NEW HAMPSHIRE

Motto: Live Free or Die

Flower: Purple Lilac   Bird: Purple Finch

Tree: White Birch

Admitted to the Union: 1788

☆

Only three years after the landing of the Pilgrims, adventurers began to move into the territory that became New Hampshire under grants from the British Crown. Seven years before Boston was founded, there was a fishing village at Portsmouth.

Fishermen and traders with the Indians discovered the richly fertile lands along the rivers. Soon farm families came to clear the virgin wilderness and to build homes. Other villages grew. People were living in most of the southern towns of New Hampshire before 1700.

The Indians were friendly at first, but they were joined by Canadian Indians after the French and Indian War broke out and the settlers suffered in many raids. Settlement was kept close to the southern border until the French and Indian War ended in 1763 and danger from the Indians was over.

Within a few years, the state was divided into towns and people were making their homes all the way up to the Canadian border. Most of the settlers were young people from the older communities to the south, and from Massachusetts and Connecticut.

They frequently named their new towns after the older places they had left, but they brought with them a pioneering desire for freedom and self-rule. New Hampshire was in a restless period of sudden growth and settlement when the troubles with Great Britain led toward war.

JOHN LANGDON

(1741–1819)

Long before most others, there were some men in New Hampshire who saw that there could be no peaceful way to solve the colony's differences with the King. They planned for the war they felt was sure to come and also planned for the statehood that would come after. One of them was John Langdon.

Sometimes called a rebel by nature, Langdon also was a man of substantial wealth and business skill who helped arouse his fellow patriots to action, fought beside them, supplied their needs of war, and then took a commanding place in the halls of legislature where the new government was formed.

Langdon's grandparents were among the first settlers of Portsmouth. He started out as an apprentice clerk in a countinghouse, but the job soon bored him and he quit to take up a life of adventure at sea. Langdon gained firsthand knowledge of the busy colonial trade and capitalized on ventures others considered risky. They brought him a handsome profit and before long he had ships of his own. He invested in land and goods and made a fortune while he was still a young man.

During visits to England, he became convinced that the King's ministers intended only evil for the colonies. From the beginning, he was one of the small band of New Hampshire patriots who called for open revolt. It wasn't a popular stand for a man of Langdon's position to take. Most New Hampshire people, especially those of Langdon's class, held back from talk of revolution.

The young royal governor, John Wentworth, had great personal popularity and was a modest and able executive. Elected to New Hampshire's last royal assembly, Langdon became Governor Wentworth's most outspoken foe. When the royal governor dissolved the assembly in 1774 because it had formed Committees of Correspondence with the other colonies, Langdon and his fellow patriots decided to hold a provincial congress of their own.

Wentworth wrote friends that Langdon dominated the state congress and that he feared any moderate course might fail. In Langdon's mind, war already seemed certain. He and the others set about arousing the people, especially in the newer settlements and country homes where they found farmers and workers ready to listen to the call.

In Boston, Paul Revere and other Massachusetts colonists had dressed themselves as Indians to dump tea into the harbor in their dramatic protest against the English taxes. There already had been small armed skirmishes with the British in New Hampshire. As public support of the patriots grew, Langdon and his group secretly planned for bold action.

They were ready for it when Paul Revere rode to Portsmouth in mid-December 1774 to warn that Britain had forbidden shipment of arms to the colonists. Acting instantly, Langdon led a raiding party against Fort William and Mary at New Castle and seized one hundred barrels of gunpowder and a store of arms from the British garrison.

The powder was carried to the home of John Sullivan, near Durham, and the captured cannon and small arms were taken to a church and to other safe hiding places.

It was one of the first open military clashes with British authority in any of the colonies, four months before the battles of Lexington and Concord. The powder and weapons that Langdon seized were used by patriots the next summer to fight the historic Battle of Bunker Hill.

Langdon was speaker of the legislature in 1775 that voted to recruit soldiers and purchase supplies. Chosen as a delegate to the Continental Congress, he helped direct the buying of goods of war for all the colonies.

The Continental Congress sent him on an unsuccessful mission to try to win Canada to the cause. After that, he was appointed an agent of Congress to seize prizes of war that ranged from gunlocks and flints to blankets and food the troops could use. During those years, he also served for awhile as a judge of New Hampshire courts, an officer of the militia, Congressional naval agent in New Hampshire, and supervisor of ship-building at Portsmouth.

With his background of seafaring adventure as a youth, Langdon was among the first to realize the value of naval operations against British ships of commerce. He helped convince the Congress of the need for an American navy. At Portsmouth, the several warships he built for the government included the famous *Ranger,* the sloop with which John Paul Jones carried the war to the very shores of the British Isles.

Meanwhile, as a leader who looked to the future in the midst of war, he helped direct sentiment in favor of free statehood. In January 1776, New Hampshire adopted a temporary colonial constitution. In June, it acted on its own authority and declared its independence of Great Britain. Three months later, it cast aside the name of colony and assumed the name State of New Hampshire.

John Langdon still was only thirty-six years old in February 1777 when he married sixteen-year-old Elizabeth Sherburne. It was an eventful year for him as speaker of the legislature and one in which he performed a service that helped to turn the whole tide of the Revolution.

Langdon personally organized and financed with his own money General John Stark's expedition against British General Burgoyne. Stark, a hero of earlier Revolutionary War battles, had returned to New Hampshire to take command of the state militia. Word was received that General Burgoyne planned to seize the colonial stores at Bennington.

This threatened invasion of New Hampshire, planned by the British as part of the Saratoga campaign, might have cut New England from communication with Washington's army. Langdon called upon his legislature to send a force of state troops under General Stark to halt Burgoyne. He pledged all his personal wealth, including his family silverware, to secure the funds needed.

"I have $3,000 in hard money," Langdon told his fellow representatives. "My plate shall be pledged for as much more. My seventy hogsheads of Tobago rum shall be sold for the most they will fetch. These are at the service of the state. If we succeed, I shall be remunerated; if not, they will be of no use to me. We can raise a brigade. Our friend Stark . . . may safely be trusted to command, and we will check Burgoyne!"

Langdon led a body of the militia in person. Within a month after that July day, General Stark had met the Hessians at Bennington, fought two decisive battles, captured or slain hundreds of Burgoyne's army, and helped to bring about the later British defeat that was considered one of the major turning points of the war. Langdon was present at the surrender of the British army at Saratoga. Later, he also commanded a detachment of New Hampshire troops in the Rhode Island campaign.

During the whole Revolution, the people were so well satisfied with the simple form of government which had been adopted that they turned down three attempts to produce a more elaborate state constitution. Langdon took a leading part in the discussions that led finally to the constitutional form of government approved in 1783. New Hampshire's constitution was largely based on the one drafted for Massachusetts.

That year, Langdon again was a delegate to the Federal Congress, then served as state senator, and in 1785 began his first term as his state's chief executive when he was elected president of New Hampshire. The following year, he was once more speaker of the legislature and, toward the close of its session, was named a delegate to the Constitutional Convention in Philadelphia.

Wartime losses had drained New Hampshire's treasury so that there wasn't enough money left to pay his expenses. Langdon offered to pay his own way and also to put up the funds for his fellow delegate, Nicholas Gilman, to make the trip. When they finally reached Philadelphia, much of the important work on the Constitution already had been done.

Langdon still was in time to argue strongly for more adequate powers for the new national government. James Madison praised him for his part in the debates over the wording of the Constitution in matters of defense, taxation and the regulation of commerce among the states.

When the convention ended, he attended another session of Congress and then hurried home to help lead the fight for ratification in New Hampshire. The government of the United States would become approved when nine of the states had accepted it and the vote in New Hampshire was to be the deciding one.

There was a feeling by many people in New Hampshire, as in some of the other states, that the new Constitution put too great power in the central government. Langdon took to the floor of the state ratifying convention, after there had been much argument, and helped to win over the delegates to his views. There was an adjournment to let the members return to their home areas to sound out public opinion, but final agreement seemed sure. In June 1788, New Hampshire became the ninth state to ratify and thus brought the United States into being.

Langdon once again served as president of the state, resigning in January to enter the United States Senate of the new government he had helped create. In the national Senate, he became temporary president throughout the First and most of the Second Congress.

In later years, he headed his state legislature, was six times re-elected governor, declined Thomas Jefferson's offer to make him Secretary of the Navy, and also turned down the Republican nomination for Vice-President. That was in 1812, when he finally retired from active politics, after having been elected to more high offices than any other man in New Hampshire's history.

"I am now seventy-one years of age," he said, "have lived the last forty years of my life in the whirlpool of politics, and am longing for the sweets of retirement."

John Langdon lived another seven years, long enough to see his beloved country victorious in the second war with England, before he died in his birthplace town of Portsmouth in 1819.

VIRGINIA

Motto: Thus Always to Tyrants

Flower: American Dogwood   Bird: Cardinal

Tree: American Dogwood

Admitted to the Union: 1788

The first permanent English settlement in the New World was at Jamestown in 1607, and Virginia became the first royal colony in 1624. Five years before it became a colony, the first representative government in America had been established in the House of Burgesses, a group of planters who met to solve problems for themselves and their neighbors.

At the time of the Revolution, Virginia had been almost self-governing for more than a century and a half. It was proud of its rights as a sovereign state and strongly rebelled against the King when he wanted to reduce those rights. Some of the greatest leaders of the Revolution came from Virginia.

But the same feelings of state pride later caused strong resentment against the idea of a powerful federal government. Virginia had the largest population of all the original states and a good living from the long-established tobacco trade. Most Virginians saw no reason why they should give up any of their privileges to an untested federal union that would allow Virginia no more voice in government than lesser states.

Some of Virginia's leaders felt that by joining forces with New York State, which was equally strong and nearly as wealthy, they could block the new Union and then make a national government that would be more to their liking.

Even if all the other states approved the Constitution and

those two held out, the Union would be divided. New York would separate the New England states from Pennsylvania, Delaware and Maryland, while Virginia would cut off North and South Carolina and Georgia from the rest.

In New York, Governor Clinton and Melancthon Smith were working for a convention they could control. They were in constant touch with Virginia's Patrick Henry, George Mason and Governor Edmund Randolph. Henry felt the new Constitution was as harmful to the liberty he cherished as the King's rule had been.

But Randolph changed sides several times during the convention that made the Constitution at Philadelphia. During the ratifying convention in Virginia, he was to change his mind once more—with far-reaching results.

EDMUND RANDOLPH
(1753–1813)

Edmund Randolph was the rebel son of a Loyalist father. He was born in 1753 at Tazewell Hall, the family's estate near Williamsburg, and grew up there. His father, uncle and grandfather all served as King's Attorneys in Virginia and his mother's father had held the same post in Maryland.

As a young lad, he met almost every important man in Virginia and many from other colonies who came to visit or dine with his father. After he graduated from the College of William and Mary, he studied law with his father.

When the royal governor fled from Virginia just before the Revolution, Edmund's father, mother and sisters left with him. Although his father had some sympathy for the patriot cause, he felt that as King's Attorney he was honor-bound to serve the Crown.

Edmund, on the threshold of his law career, stayed behind and moved to an uncle's home. That summer, he journeyed to Cambridge, Massachusetts, and offered his services to General Washington. Edmund became Washington's aide-de-camp until his uncle's death made it necessary for him to return to Williamsburg.

Practicing law in the once-colonial capital of Virginia, he sought the company of other young men who openly favored breaking Virginia's ties with England. His ready knowledge of colonial law, learned from his Loyalist father, qualified him to be the youngest member-delegate to Virginia's first convention in 1776 to frame a state constitution.

Edmund became the state's first attorney general under the new constitution and also mayor of Williamsburg and a delegate to the Continental Congress. He was a man who wanted to be liked and he enjoyed the popularity that came to leaders of the revolt against England. As a lawyer, he was fascinated by the emerging form of government and felt that all the states eventually would have to join in a union stronger than the one they had under the Articles of Confederation.

Elected Virginia's governor in 1786, he attended the first convention of delegates from the various states who met at Annapolis, Maryland, to form a better union, and later was a delegate to the Philadelphia convention that framed the Constitution. As one of George Washington's legal advisers, he helped convince the retired general that despite his personal wishes Washington should re-enter public life and take part in the Philadelphia convention.

The Virginia delegates were the first to arrive at Philadelphia. They held their own meetings while they waited for enough delegates to get there from the other states. All the Virginians had wide experience in politics and they agreed that if they worked out the first definite plan to present to the members at the opening of the convention, it not only would provide something to build upon, but also probably would have the best chance of passage.

They put on paper what became known as the Virginia Plan. Drawn largely from James Madison's vast knowledge of the world's history of constitutional law, it also reflected Randolph's legal ideals.

Once the plan was complete, the Virginians had to decide who would present it. Washington naturally was the first choice, but it seemed likely he would be the convention's president. Randolph, as governor, held the highest political position in the group and was both handsome in manner and practiced at public speaking.

He offered the Virginia Plan as the first major speaker after the opening business of the convention. There was immediate dispute. Other states also had plans for the national government, many of them far more conservative than a complete new constitution. Some openly opposed strong federal union. Others, especially the smaller states, feared big and rich Virginia and mistrusted any plan Virginia wanted.

By nature, Randolph wasn't a man to accept criticism easily or to give in willingly to compromise. He resisted the efforts to broaden the new Constitution to please a majority of the delegates. There were so many changes by the time the convention had finished the final draft that he was flatly against it and refused to sign.

Madison and other Federalists were shocked and alarmed by Randolph's change of heart. The popular young governor controlled a great many votes. There were rumors that he planned to join with New York's Governor Clinton, who also had refused to sign, to try to withhold the two strongest states from the Union.

On his return home from Philadelphia, Randolph sent a letter to the Virginia legislature, explaining his reasons for not signing the Constitution. He set to work with Patrick Henry and other Anti-Federalists campaigning against having Virginia ratify it. But as the time for Virginia to act grew closer, he became less outspoken.

When Virginia's convention met to vote on the new document, Patrick Henry opened debate for those against it. He asked by what authority the writers of the Constitution had spoken for "We the people" instead of "We the states."

Randolph stood next and everybody expected him to strengthen Patrick Henry's opening arguments. But Randolph had changed his mind once more. There were gasps of surprise when he declared it was too late to argue over what the Constitution should have been.

Dramatically, he pointed out that since eight states already were known to have approved, Virginia's only choice was union or no union at all. Randolph said he would consent to chopping off his arm before he would agree to dissolving the Union.

The Federalists were jubilant over Randolph's return to their side. Bewildered opponents of the Constitution, stunned by his about-face, questioned his reasons and even suggested that he had been blackmailed or was hoping for personal gain. After one bitter exchange of personal insults on the floor, Patrick Henry and Randolph were close to a duel, but friends of both convinced them to call it off.

Randolph did more than merely change his mind. He delayed making public a letter that might have kept Virginia from ratifying the Constitution. The letter was from New York's Governor Clinton and it implied that if Virginia refused to vote for the Constitution as it stood, so would New York.

One governor couldn't ignore such a letter from another governor. But Randolph held it on his desk until the day Virginia was to give the vote on the Constitution. He then delivered it to the legislature for consideration, but it wasn't read to the state's lawmakers that day because all the members were busy with the convention's final debates.

Virginia approved the Constitution by a slim margin of ten votes. At the time, Virginians thought that theirs had become the ninth and deciding state to ratify. Word wasn't received until three days later that New Hampshire already had acted and thus had taken the honor of bringing the United States into being.

Edmund Randolph afterward became the nation's Secretary of State and also enjoyed a busy and profitable law practice which included acting as an attorney for Aaron Burr during his trial for treason. He died in 1813 at the age of sixty.

NEW YORK

Motto: Excelsior (Ever Upward)

Flower: Rose

Bird: Eastern Bluebird

Tree: Sugar Maple

Admitted to the Union: 1788

☆

New York and the Hudson River had been sighted by some of the early English and Spanish explorers, but it was first settled by the Dutch who established the villages and farms.

The English, who had settled in neighboring lands, moved in and took control of the capital of New Amsterdam in 1664. Charles II, then King of England, granted the area to his brother, the Duke of York. The English set up a limited form of self-government in which the Dutch settlers shared.

Early in the eighteenth century freedom of the press was determined in an important court case in New York. Peter Zenger had been arrested for libel and the lawyer who succeeded in defending him also established the right of newspapers to print the truth. New York's free press played a vital part in its struggle toward independence and statehood.

Many decisive Revolutionary War battles were fought in the colony and New York City was invaded and held by the British until the war ended. The English hoped to cut off New England from the rest of the colonies by taking all of New York State, but this was stopped when the colonists won the battle of Saratoga.

New York would have provided a natural division of the new country if it had been held in enemy hands. Later, Governor Clinton and others who disliked the way the Constitution was written tried to divide the states politically, just as the war itself might have divided them, by keeping New York from approving it.

ALEXANDER HAMILTON
(*1757–1804*)

On an October night in 1787, aboard the ship he frequently took from the capital at Albany to New York City where he lived and practiced law, Alexander Hamilton sat at a table in his cabin and wrote a letter. He often worked during the trip and this particular letter was one that would be published in a newspaper under a pen name.

It was addressed to Governor Clinton, archfoe of the Constitution. The two men had exchanged other letters that were published for the public to read, Clinton writing his over the name Cato and Hamilton replying by signing his Caesar. But since many people thought of Caesar as a tyrant, Hamilton this time chose a different pen name. With a flourish, he signed the letter Publius, and when the ship docked, he dispatched it to the *New York Journal.*

The letter was the first of eighty-four more that were to come, some written by James Madison, a few by John Jay, but most of them by Hamilton. All were signed Publius and almost all were written with equal haste, sometimes with a printer's messenger leaning over the desk to snatch them from Hamilton's hand. After the whole series had been printed in the paper, they were collected and bound into a booklet.

Some fifty copies of the little booklet were sent to Madison in Virginia to help him convince the delegates at Virginia's state convention that they should ratify the Constitution. The rest of the copies were distributed in Clinton's stronghold of Anti-Federalism, New York State.

As a piece of political propaganda, the booklet wasn't much of a success. But the papers, titled *The Federalist,* became a guide to the meaning of the Constitution and probably will endure as long as that historic document itself.

Years before, when he was just a boy, Hamilton's talent as a writer had won him the chance to come to America. As a teen-ager living in the West Indies, he was impressed by the violence of a hurricane in the islands. He wrote a vivid account of the storm and sent it to the *Royal Danish-American Gazette* of St. Croix. To the delight of his youthful pride, the paper published it.

He was so highly praised for his writing ability that his aunts, as well as other relatives and some interested teachers and friends, pooled their resources to send him to America to college. While he was in New York attending King's College (now Columbia University), he made friends with other young liberals who were rebellious against British rule.

Hamilton joined the militia in 1775, took part in many New York and New Jersey battles, and became an aide to General Washington. He asked Washington to let him command a battalion, but Washington didn't want to lose his services because Hamilton was so valuable to him.

Washington refused the request, but Hamilton still was anxious to get back into more active fighting. Soon after his marriage to beautiful Elizabeth Schuyler, he resigned from Washington's staff and finally was given command of a light infantry battalion. Hamilton's troops broke through the British defenses in Virginia in 1781 in the campaign that led to the surrender of Cornwallis at Yorktown.

After the war, having been admitted to the bar following only three months of intensive study, Hamilton took up his law practice, became a receiver of taxes and was chosen a delegate to the Continental Congress. At the Annapolis convention in 1786, he drafted the resolution that called for a meeting in Philadelphia to enlarge the powers of the Federal Government.

The next year, by then a member of New York's state assembly, Hamilton also was a delegate to the Constitutional Convention at Philadelphia, along with Robert Yates and John Lansing.

In many ways, the document that came out of the debates during that long, hot summer in Philadelphia was far from Hamilton's own ideas as to how a stronger national government should be formed. But he felt that the Constitution offered a plan that would work and probably was the best compromise all the parties would accept. Both Yates and Lansing, strong Anti-Federalists, had left the convention early. The only New York name signed to the document was Alexander Hamilton's.

Governor Clinton, as the leader of those against the Constitution, kept putting off the call for a New York state convention to ratify it. Hamilton and the other Federalists in the New York assembly finally forced a bill through both houses by a very slim margin. Clinton then called for a general vote of the people to elect delegates and the Federalists had to agree to it.

The state was overwhelmingly against the Constitution and the delegates opposed to ratification outnumbered the Federalists by more than two to one. Hamilton's men were elected in New York City, but that was the only Federalist stronghold in the state.

When Hamilton arrived at Poughkeepsie, where the New York convention was being held, he knew that the only thing in his favor would be time. The New Hampshire and Virginia conventions were in session and if either of those states ratified, the Constitution would go into effect, with or without New York. Hamilton had asked both states to send him the results at once, by relays of fast horses, as soon as any decision was reached.

The New Yorkers against the Constitution wanted their convention to vote as soon as possible. They had a clear majority and most of them saw no reason to go over the document in detail since they were going to turn it down anyhow. But Hamilton stalled for time and sought to have the Constitution taken up clause by clause.

One of those then opposed to it was Melancthon Smith. Proud of his debating abilities, Smith felt he could outtalk any of the Federalists, even Hamilton, and convince them that

64

the Constitution was wrong for New York. Governor Clinton later said that it was this "vanity that lost us the cause." But the New York convention finally agreed to debate each separate part of the document.

Point by point, the articles were brought up. Day by day, Hamilton spoke at length in their favor. He quoted the *Federalist* papers so often he was asked if he was making up a second version. His long speeches amounted to a filibuster, in which he kept going back over the same things, with nearly the same words, again and again, but always clearly explaining the points in question.

He was waiting for the first messenger from New Hampshire or Virginia. The New Yorkers' tempers were growing short. Most of the delegates remained unconvinced by his arguments. There were many quarrels, threats of duels, and a riot one night by impatient crowds on the main streets of Poughkeepsie.

Presiding over the meeting, Governor Clinton had come to agree with Melancthon Smith that the Federalists should have their full say so the quarrels would end when the vote went against them, as Clinton confidently expected that it finally would.

At last, the message came from New Hampshire. The ninth state had ratified. "The Constitution is now in force," Hamilton proclaimed from the floor. "Nine states will form a union without us."

"Let them try it," Governor Clinton answered, "and we'll see if it works."

So far as Hamilton knew, not one man in that New York convention had been swayed by his arguments. Long weeks of debate seemingly had changed nothing. Hamilton and the Federalists called for the convention to adjourn. They threatened to act without the rest of the state, to let the upstate counties do as they pleased while they went home and worked for New York City and the surrounding southern area to secede from the state and enter the Union on its own.

Their motion for adjournment was defeated. Governor

Clinton called at last for the vote. As Hamilton sat listening to the roll call, he fully expected defeat.

Then Melancthon Smith's name was called. To Hamilton's great surprise, the man who had been so proudly certain he could outdebate him announced that Hamilton's arguments had convinced him. Instead of voting against the Constitution, Smith voted for it, with the provision that Congress should speedily adopt certain amendments.

Others followed Smith's lead, agreeing to qualified approval. When the final count was taken, the New York convention voted to join the Union by only three votes. The unexpected decision was thirty to twenty-seven in favor of the Constitution.

With the Union established, Hamilton went on to become the first Secretary of the Treasury, serving until 1795. He was a member of Congress in 1801 when the presidential election was thrown into the House of Representatives for a decision because Thomas Jefferson and Aaron Burr had received an equal number of electoral votes. Although he and Jefferson were political enemies, Hamilton finally voted for Jefferson because he considered Burr a dangerous man.

He and Burr had been at constant odds in New York politics. Hamilton called him a man of greedy ambition and frequently denounced him. Burr blamed Hamilton for his political defeats and demanded satisfaction on the field of honor. When Hamilton refused to take back his unflattering statements, Burr challenged Hamilton to a duel.

Facing the thought of possible death, Hamilton wanted to set his affairs in order. There was one secret he was unwilling to carry with him to the grave, but it was not his alone to reveal. The authorship of the *Federalist* papers had been anonymous and was to remain so. Only Washington had known who the authors were and he by then was dead.

Hamilton was proud of those papers. He had heard them quoted by the Supreme Court as the ultimate authority on the Constitution and he wanted future generations to know his part in them. The morning before the duel, he called at the home of an old and trusted friend.

The friend was out and Hamilton waited as long as he could, but he would trust his secret to nobody else. He took a piece of paper from his pocket and wrote a brief message on it. Then he slipped the paper into a book that he knew his friend would open.

When it was found later, the cryptic message bore a list of numbers opposite the initials, H, M and J. Hamilton had recalled, to the best of his knowledge after more than a decade, which of the *Federalist* papers had been written by Madison, Jay and himself.

At dawn on July 11, 1804, he met Burr on the lofty palisades of Weehawken, New Jersey. Mortally wounded, Hamilton was rowed back across the Hudson and died the next day at a doctor's home. But Alexander Hamilton's fame continued to live, not only in the memory of his state-making deeds, but also everlastingly as the principal author of *The Federalist*.

NORTH CAROLINA

Motto: To Be, Rather Than To Seem

Flower: Dogwood   Bird: Cardinal

Admitted to the Union: 1789

Roanoke Island, off the coast of North Carolina, was the site of the first planned English colony in America and the locale of one of early America's mysteries.

A whole colony of English settlers who landed there in 1587 disappeared completely, leaving not a single clue as to what happened to them, except for the unexplained word CROATAN that was found carved in a tree.

Later on, some people moved in from Virginia, but the natural handicaps of shallow rivers and marshy land made settlement slow. By 1700 the population of the whole area was only about four thousand. After North Carolina was made a royal colony, more settlers came and trade was established with other coastal cities and with Bermuda.

However, because it was difficult for people in one part of the colony to communicate with those in another section, the coastal settlers and upcountry farmers remained divided and two separate political viewpoints grew. During the Revolution, the two groups were almost as much in dispute with each other as they were with the British.

The clash of viewpoints led to further troubles when North Carolina moved toward statehood.

JAMES IREDELL
(1751–1799)

James Iredell was a maker, keeper and explainer of laws that built a state. He was a believer in liberty who also believed in the need for strong government by law to preserve that liberty, and he helped North Carolina understand the need.

Born in England, the son of a Bristol merchant, Iredell was only seventeen when he was sent to North Carolina to serve as comptroller of customs. During the six years he held the post, he also managed the New World business interests of an uncle.

As a popular young bachelor, he enjoyed the social life of Edenton. But although he was a fun-loving young man, he also had a more serious side. Already well educated, he devoted himself to reading every book he could find. He soon saw a richer future for himself in law than in business and he set about studying it under the region's leading lawyer, Samuel Johnston.

Johnston had studied in England with the great English lawyer Blackstone, and from him Iredell received an unusually fine understanding of the basic reasoning of law. Iredell qualified for the bar in 1771 and two years later married his teacher's young sister, Hannah Johnston.

As a man who had served the Crown as a collector of customs, Iredell began to feel strongly that new British taxes against the colonies were unjust. He wrote his views in published letters that gained the attention of patriot leaders. But Iredell urged calm reasoning to bring about fair treatment. Even in the spring of 1776 when armed revolt seemed certain, he still hoped for a peaceful settlement.

When the final break with England came, North Carolina was left with a hastily established government that had no real legal basis. Iredell was chosen to help draft new laws and revise the old ones so they would suit the new state. He also helped to re-establish the courts, which had ceased to function, and served as a judge of the superior court for six months. In 1779, he became North Carolina's attorney general.

After the Revolution, as a member of the Council of State, he was appointed by the legislature to collect and revise all the acts then in force, a task which took him four years to finish. While he was busy giving North Carolina the foundation of law upon which its government could stand, Iredell also took a vital interest in what was being done in Philadelphia to create a nation of constitutional government.

There were not many North Carolinians who agreed with him that his state must become part of a stronger federal union. Everywhere, he heard criticism of the new Constitution. Iredell felt that many of those who were against it didn't really understand that the Union would insure their hard-won freedom instead of destroying it. He answered the critics in a pamphlet published under the pen name of Marcus.

The little pamphlet was welcomed by Federalists in the other colonies and brought Iredell's talent to the attention of George Washington, but it did little to change the minds of the upcountry people of his own state.

When North Carolina held its first convention to decide whether to ratify the Constitution, Iredell led the debates to support it as a representative from his home borough of Edenton. Known as a man of great tact and personal charm, he needed all of it as floor leader for the outnumbered Federalists.

Just as Madison and Hamilton had done in Virginia and New York, Iredell patiently defended each section of the document. But when it came to the vote, North Carolina refused to ratify. Only eighty-four delegates were for the Constitution and one hundred eighty-four were against it.

Iredell refused to admit defeat. He just couldn't believe that the people of his state understood the principles involved. If he could somehow reach them, explain to them, carry the arguments directly to the people themselves instead of to their representatives, he was sure logical reasoning would prevail and they would see the worth of the Constitution.

Some of his companions called him an impractical idealist. They said he had too much faith in the intelligence of the people, that he was dealing with opponents who were mostly uneducated and that all the reasoning in the world would never change their minds. But Iredell couldn't be shaken from that faith in the ability of the people to reason. It was the strength upon which the whole new democracy rested.

He had the debates of the convention published. With the help of a friend, he had copies distributed throughout the state. He also saw to it that statewide publicity was given to the ten amendments the national Congress added to the Constitution during it first session.

Iredell helped convince the people that the Constitution, as amended, now guaranteed their personal liberties. The news brought immediate reaction. People demanded another convention. On November 19, 1789, North Carolina's second ratification convention voted to accept the Constitution by one hundred ninety-four votes to seventy-seven.

President Washington named Iredell to the Supreme Court. He was the youngest of the Justices, still only thirty-eight years old. In those early years of the Supreme Court, the duties of a Justice included presiding at various courthouses in his own district. Iredell rode the circuit, through the swamps and the woods and in all kinds of weather.

He described his own life as that "of a post boy in a circuit of vast extent, under great difficulties of travel and perils of life in the sickly season." The exhausting work undermined his health and he died only two weeks after his forty-eighth birthday at his home in Edenton. But James Iredell had lived to see his state become part of a Union based on laws made by the will of the people.

RHODE ISLAND

Motto: Hope

Flower: Violet   Bird: Rhode Island Red

Tree: Red Maple

Admitted to the Union: 1790

☆

Roger Williams founded Providence in 1636 on land bought from the Indians. He had been banished from Massachusetts by the Puritans because of his liberal views as a minister and teacher. The settlement became a haven for those forced to flee from England and Holland because of religious and political beliefs.

Soon there were other settlements and Williams secured a patent from the British Parliament under which four towns drew up a code of laws and organized a government in 1647. The settlements quarreled among themselves, broke apart, and came back into one government again under a liberal royal charter granted by King Charles II.

For years Rhode Island was looked down upon by its wealthier and more powerful neighbor colonies. Most of the early settlers were farmers, fishermen and Indian traders, strongly independent men who had little sympathy for any government that tried to tell them what to do. Each separate town was fiercely jealous of its own rights.

Common resentment against the British led the Rhode Islanders to declare their independence two months before the rest of America. But when the Revolution was won, most Rhode Islanders were against joining in a government with the other states.

Rhode Island held out against ratifying the Constitution

until 1790. Times had changed by then so there was more industry with business interests outside the state. Faced with money troubles and a threat by the Federal Congress to cut its revenues, Rhode Island reluctantly became one of the United States by a margin of two votes. But the state government continued under the old colonial charter until a new state constitution was adopted in 1843.

JOHN BROWN

(1736–1803)

Eight small boats quietly slipped away from the shore south of Providence on a June night in 1772. The men aboard included some of the city's leading merchants. In the darkness, they rowed out into Narragansett Bay. Ahead of them was the hulking shadow of the British revenue cutter *Gaspee* which had been lured to run aground in the shallows while chasing another vessel that afternoon.

For three months the *Gaspee* and her harsh captain had been trying to enforce the hated British revenue laws that were defied by American patriots who took to smuggling goods ashore rather than obey the dictates of the Crown.

The small boats edged close in the hush of night. Suddenly the leader of the raiding party, a bold young giant of a man, gave the signal to attack. The men scrambled aboard the armed British schooner.

In the flurry of gunfire, the captain was wounded. The crew, taken completely by surprise, was forced to surrender. The patriot raiders put captain and crew ashore and then set fire to the *Gaspee*. As they rowed away they watched it burn to ruin.

The infuriated British offered a reward of a thousand pounds for information that would prove who had led the raid. They suspected John Brown, partner with his brothers in a mercantile business that had dealings around the world, and they threatened to send him to England to be tried for treason. But they had no proof. The hostile Rhode Islanders would tell them nothing.

Hearings were held in two sessions of public inquiry that lasted for months before the case was dropped for lack of evidence. It wasn't until after the Revolution began that the full story was told of Brown's leadership during that night of defiance when the *Gaspee* was burned.

John Brown was three years old when his merchant father died, leaving him and his brothers to be brought up by their mother. She was a woman of forceful character, who taught her son to stand up for the things in which he believed. As a young man, he already had begun to show the boldness of thought and action that made him a leader in the cause for independence and one of those who later helped move reluctant Rhode Island into the union of federal states.

Brown was active in the state assembly that opposed the Stamp Act. He helped arouse other merchants to ban imports of British goods. When open warfare with the British began, he took part in ousting the governor for refusing to raise troops.

He was outspokenly on the side of free statehood, using his influence to encourage the act of Rhode Island independence that was passed in May 1776. Two months later, he helped the general assembly to resolve that "the style and title of this government . . . shall be the State of Rhode Island and Providence Plantations."

Already, Brown and his brothers were dealing with a secret committee of the Continental Congress to supply Revolutionary troops with clothing and weapons of war. As merchants, they had international standing, with vital contacts that reached from the West Indies to London, Marseilles, Copenhagen and Hamburg. Brown put them to full use, along with the company's ships, in serving the American forces, as the records of their secret negotiations with Congress later revealed.

He was named to a committee to oversee the work of building American ships of war and he also built and outfitted privateers that harassed the British at sea. At home, he and his brothers developed the state's iron manufacturing industry so as to use ore dug from pits at Cranston. Their plant, Furnace Hope, turned out cannon of sizes up to eighteen-pounders for the Revolution.

When financial hard times came to Rhode Island after the war, Brown was accused by some of his townsmen of having been a profiteer who rode the wave of patriotism to his own advantage. Even those who criticized him during the general depression of the postwar years admitted his personal courage and daring.

He did become a very wealthy man, but his foresight in developing new trade and industry also helped bring wealth and prosperity to his state. In 1787 his firm sent out the first Providence vessel to engage in direct trade with the East Indies and China.

The ship, the *General Washington,* cleared for the East with a cargo of locally made goods and returned a year and a half later with tea, silks, china, cloves and other riches worth three times as much. It was the start of trading with the Orient that continued to bring fortune to Rhode Island for more than half a century.

Brown's home in Providence was described by John Quincy Adams as the most magnificent and elegant mansion in all New England. It was the scene of many fashionable balls and other social functions. It also was a place where men of power and influence planned the political strategy they hoped would bring Rhode Island into closer union with the other colonies.

Although he seldom held important political office himself, except for his election as a non-attending delegate to the Federal Congress in 1784 and again in 1785, Brown was a leader of those men of great influence. His friendships, his position in the business world and his wealth and social prominence, all helped add weight to his words.

When the Constitutional Convention was held at Philadelphia in 1787, those who opposed strong federal government were in control of the state. Rhode Island ignored the convention and refused to send a delegation.

Brown and the group he and his brothers helped to lead, mostly men of commercial interests, made a determined effort to have the legislators call a state convention on the issue. But the Anti-Federalists, mainly from rural farming areas, feared they would have to sacrifice too many of their state rights to the national government. They swung the balance of power that turned down a state convention.

Instead, they proposed a statewide vote on the question. The Federalists refused to take part in it. Rhode Island had some 6,000 eligible voters at the time. Only about half of them cast ballots. The result was that, in all Rhode Island, there were only 237 votes in favor of the Constitution.

Brown and his group devoted themselves to changing the public mind and, more importantly, the minds of the politicians. His own success with his shipping and manufacturing ventures, meanwhile, was changing the state from a farming to an industrial one. This also helped some voters to see that their future lay in strong federal union which would reach for added trade far beyond the farms.

The Federal Congress tried to force Rhode Island into the Union by placing it outside the revenue limits of the rest of the country and set 1790 as a deadline for enforcing the act. A Rhode Island convention finally met in South Kingstown in March of that year, but adjourned without coming to a decision. Two months later, a second convention met at Newport and ratified the Constitution by the narrow vote of thirty-four to thirty-two.

Brown served one term in Congress, from 1799 to 1801. Years previously, he had laid the cornerstone of what became Brown University. In his late years, he retired from political activity but was still a prominent figure in the community, a huge old man whose bulk "took up a whole chaise seat ordinarily occupied by two." He died at the age of sixty-seven in 1803.

The thirteen original states agreed to admit new states into the Union by vote of Congress. Power to decide whether a new state should be admitted was given Congress by Article IV, Section 3, of the Constitution. It also declared that no new state should be formed within the jurisdiction of any other state, or by joining parts of states, without the consent of the legislatures of the states concerned, as well as of the Congress.

Some new states had to obtain the consent of older states to separate their lands from those states, before they could ask Congress to admit them to the Union. Other new states were formed of territories created out of the Western lands controlled by Congress.

The formula for creating territories and then new states was set by the old Congress of Confederation in 1787, when it formed the Northwest Territory out of Western lands ceded to the Federal Government by the original states. The Ordinance of 1787, adopted by the Congress of Confederation while the Constitution was still being considered, outlined the plan generally followed when later territories were created and then became states.

It called for the appointment of a territorial governor, a secretary, and three judges, who were to control the area until the voting population reached 5,000 citizens. Then the people could elect a legislature and send a non-voting Representative to Washington. When the population reached 60,000 or more, the territory could apply to Congress to be admitted as a state.

PART II. ACROSS THE MOUNTAINS

VERMONT

Motto: Freedom and Unity

Flower: Red Clover   Bird: Hermit Thrush

Tree: Sugar Maple

Admitted to the Union: 1791

☆

Vermont was an independent republic for nearly fourteen years. It fought off the claims of its neighbors to win acceptance as a separate state. During the years when Congress refused to take it into the Union, Vermont governed itself as a small nation with sovereign rights.

It coined money, raised its own armed forces, established post offices, naturalized citizens of other states and countries, corresponded with foreign governments and appointed envoys to other powers.

Until about thirty years before the Revolution, much of Vermont was practically an unsettled wilderness. A fort had been built there earlier by Massachusetts to protect its western settlements. Connecticut also laid claim to some of the lands of what was first New Connecticut and later Verde-Mont. The name was coined from French words that meant "Green Mountain."

But the real trouble that kept Vermont so long from being accepted as a state started with a boundary dispute between New York and New Hampshire when both were royal colonies. Lands sold to settlers under the New Hampshire grants later were claimed by New York.

When New York tried to throw out the old grants and to make new ones for the same land, some Vermonters took up arms to fight the Yorkers. Throughout the Revolution, Vermont patriots held off not only the British, but also the attempts of neighboring colonies to swallow up the newborn state.

THOMAS CHITTENDEN
(1730–1797)

It was a one-eyed giant of a man who shrewdly and cleverly led Vermont along its own road to independence. He was Thomas Chittenden, chief executive of Vermont during almost all the years it was a separate republic. Chittenden helped the loyal Vermonters stand up to the American Congress, to neighbor colonies and to the British enemy, and gradually won his state a place in the Union.

He looked and acted like a simple, unschooled farmer. But his friendly, easygoing country manner often took in those who came against him and they sometimes learned to their surprise that he was much smarter than he seemed. He relished the life of a pioneer, and beneath his bland appearance and outward calm he was a daring adventurer, a bold statesman, and an experienced politician with a keen and crafty brain.

Born in East Guilford, Connecticut, he went to a small rural school as a boy, but had very little formal education. When he was eighteen he took to sea as a sailor aboard a merchant ship bound for the West Indies. It was captured by the French and Chittenden was several years working his passage back to Connecticut.

For a long time his desire for adventure seemed satisfied. He gave up the sea and settled down near the Connecticut town of Salisbury to become a farmer as his father had been before him. He married, became a respected landowner, and devoted himself to farming for almost twenty-five years. But his seafaring youth had taught him more about the outside world and the men in it than most of his land-bound neighbors.

In Salisbury he gained political experience, too. He was a justice of the peace and six times was chosen a representative to the colonial legislature. One of his neighbors was Ethan Allen, later leader of the Green Mountain Boys, who had gone to Vermont to speculate in land sales there. Chittenden was caught up in the excitement of his friend's pioneering and by the reports of the fertile river-valley land that could be bought cheaply and which offered new settlers rich opportunity.

He sold his farm in Connecticut and bought land in Vermont from Allen. The property was part of the grants that had been made by New Hampshire. Chittenden moved there and soon became a leader among other farmers of the area in their struggles against the Yorkers. He was the only man for miles around who had ever been a member of a colonial legislature, although he later claimed ignorance of the way such assemblies should be conducted and sometimes violated all the rules to get some vital measure adopted without fuss and red tape.

Less than two years after he moved to Vermont, Chittenden helped to write the first documents calling for a separate government. His neighboring farmers chose him to represent them at a convention held in Dorset. Delegates to that meeting in 1776 approved Articles of Association that were to be submitted to town meetings throughout the area of the New Hampshire Grants.

The Articles declared loyalty to the new United States, but also called for a government that would be independent of New York or other states. Although a few towns objected to breaking relations with New York, most of them approved the Articles.

Another meeting of delegates promptly acted to abolish the remaining New York laws, to put the militia under the convention's command, and to appoint a committee to seek admission to the Union. New York was having troubles of its own with the British and took little official notice at first of what was happening in Vermont.

Under Chittenden's leadership, a convention met at Westminster in 1777 and formally declared its independence. He and four others drew up the declaration that was swiftly and unanimously approved. In its form, it followed the Declaration of Independence, but clearly stated the reasons for separating from New York.

The convention declared: "That the district of land commonly called and known by the name of the New Hampshire Grants be a new and separate state and for the future conduct themselves as such" and that it "ought to be and hereby is declared forever and hereafter to be considered a separate, free and independent jurisdiction."

New York treated the act as beneath its notice and tried to ignore it by adopting in its own constitution a rule that would have wiped out the titles of ownership of many of the farmers who held land under the royal grants. Meanwhile, the Continental Congress refused to recognize Vermont's secession from New York.

In Vermont, Chittenden and the others went right ahead and framed their own constitution for the infant state. It set up a republic, allowed all men the right to vote, and provided that until the new government was established the affairs of the republic were to be managed by a Council of Safety, to which Chittenden was named a member.

The Constitution had hardly been approved when the British invaded. Neighbors of the new Vermont Republic sent it no help. Without arms, ammunition or money to pay for either, the harried Council of Safety led a wretched existence. Fighting against the enemy to defend their homes, the Vermonters also had to fight the claims of New York and political groups within the area that wanted to make it part of New Hampshire or Massachusetts.

Nevertheless, the new legislature met and when votes were counted, Chittenden had been elected Vermont's first governor. The representatives had no time, in the midst of all their troubles, to make a code of laws. They voted that Vermont should be governed by the laws of God and Connecticut "until we have time to frame better."

Chittenden, outwardly the simple and easygoing farmer, managed by his skillful political maneuvering to win over one faction after another and keep the new state together. He blocked petitions to divide it, to annex it to other states, to destroy the already formed republic and create new and independent splinter states.

He quieted revolts that threatened to burst into open rioting. With all his powers of persuasion, Chittenden tried to calm neighboring New Hampshire, which had been angered because some of its border towns wanted to join Vermont. There were rumors that the Continental Congress was ready "to annihilate the state of Vermont" and that New Hampshire and New York plotted to divide Vermont between them.

New York appealed to Congress to uphold its claims to the territory. Congress sent investigators to Vermont and Chittenden dealt with them cleverly. He was friendly, but firm in making them understand that his new state would not surrender to New York. He let the emissaries from Congress think that if they pushed Vermont too far, it might go over to the side of the British. The same bluff worked later with the British themselves, when Vermont leaders entered into secret negotiations that led the British to hold back military action.

Chittenden wrote to John Jay, President of Congress, that any armed attempt by New York to enforce rule over Vermont would be met by Vermont troops. Congress, however, looked upon Vermont not as a state, but as a place where political disputes had "risen so high as to endanger the internal peace of the United States." And Congress prepared to end the self-proclaimed state.

Congress asked New York, New Hampshire and Massachusetts to pass laws that would give the national government the right to settle jurisdiction over the contested land. It forbade the Vermont government to issue any more property grants and restricted the collection of revenues. New York and New Hampshire immediately voted to let Congress decide. Massachusetts notified Congress that it had a "clear and indisputable right" to the southeastern part of the area that had called itself Vermont.

Before Congress could act, the Vermont legislature met and informed the world that since it had not been admitted to the Union, Congress had no authority over it. The delegates declared that Vermont was a wholly free and independent republic. Defying Congress, Chittenden and his group decided that Vermont should go right ahead and sell grants of land.

Congress was faced with the fact that the only way to take over the area would be by open warfare. It had enough on its hands in fighting the British. Meanwhile, leaders of the Vermont Republic were busy appealing to the other colonies to support its struggle for independence.

Although Congress proclaimed that Vermont's conduct was "highly unwarrantable and subversive to the peace and welfare of the United States," it took no action. Chittenden repeated the threat that Vermont might side with the British. In a letter to Congress, he said that since Vermont was refused the right to become one of the United States, then certainly the republic "was at liberty to offer or accept terms for cessation of hostilities with Great Britain."

Congress was rocked by the possibility that Vermont, keystone to defenses of the northern frontier, might quit the war. The delegates at Philadelphia were further shocked when envoys from Vermont, allowed to attend the sessions only as spectators, said that under the circumstances they didn't want to be there at all. The Vermonters turned their backs on Congress and went home.

The result was that Congress avoided making any immediate decision. Vermont's republic was allowed to live, but Congress repeatedly turned down its bids to be made a state. Chittenden gradually won over Massachusetts and New Hampshire and he went to work, behind the scenes, on the politicians in New York.

When the first Congress to assemble under the new Constitution met in New York in 1789, Alexander Hamilton favored admission of Vermont to strengthen the Federalist Party.

George Washington, who once had felt that Vermont might have to be subdued with force, also looked more favorably on granting statehood. Vermont had been waiting for years and Congress finally offered to welcome it into the family.

New York had called Chittenden many names and never had referred to him as a governor. But the New York legislature, in July 1789, addressed him for the first time as "Your Excellency," in offering to negotiate the old land claims. The Vermont Republic agreed to pay $30,000 and New York withdrew all opposition to Vermont's admission to the Union.

Chittenden presided at the convention held in Bennington in 1791 to ratify the Constitution of the United States and make formal petition for statehood. There still were some Vermonters satisfied with things as they were. They wanted Vermont to go on as a republic. They debated loudly and, right to the end, four delegates were against joining the Union.

Most of them listened to the calming wisdom of the old man who had led the republic through its long struggle for recognition as a state. Under Chittenden's leadership, they ratified. One month later, Washington signed the act that made Vermont the fourteenth of the United States.

Thomas Chittenden, the adventurous farmer who had been chief executive of the little Vermont Republic, became governor of the state and remained in that office for six more years before his death at the age of sixty-seven.

KENTUCKY

Motto: United We Stand, Divided We Fall
Flower: Goldenrod   Bird: Cardinal
Tree: Tulip Tree
Admitted to the Union: 1792

☆

The barrier of the mountains kept settlers out of what became
Kentucky until just before the Revolution. It was land specu-
lator Richard Henderson who really opened the area to settlement. He was a Virginian who had become a judge in North
Carolina. Long interested in developing western lands that
could be sold to colonists, he was the chief promoter of the
Transylvania Company. Henderson paid the Cherokee Indians ten thousand pounds for land that made up nearly all
of Kentucky.

He hired Daniel Boone and a party of thirty men to clear
and mark a wagon road from Cumberland Gap to the place
on the Kentucky River where Boonesboro was founded in the
spring of 1775. Settlers who came over Boone's Wilderness
Road into the lands sold by Henderson's company soon chose
delegates to meet in the first legislative assembly west of the
Alleghenies. Called together by Henderson, they drew up a
code of laws for the "colony of Transylvania."

The land company tried to get Virginia and North Carolina
to approve the grants and even petitioned the Federal Congress to have Transylvania admitted as a state. Congress refused because, as John Adams put it, "these proprietors have
no grant from the Crown, nor from any Colony; are within
the limits of Virginia and North Carolina by their charters

and . . . are charged with republican notions and Utopian schemes."

Virginia voided the company's claims, although settlers were allowed to keep title to their grants. But the country had been opened up and the vanguard of families from Virginia sent back glowing reports of the fertile farmland the other side of the mountains. When the Revolution ended, hundreds of returning soldiers swelled the tide of those adventuring westward from the older colonies.

ISAAC SHELBY
(1750–1826)

The shaping of Kentucky into a state required pathfinders and surveyors to map the wilderness land, soldiers to fight the Indians, and military leaders to battle in the cause of independence. It also required lawmakers to form its new government and statesmen to guide it.

All these needs were met in one person in Isaac Shelby, pioneer surveyor, patriot commander, and first governor. Like his father before him, he achieved great fame as a warrior against the Indians as well as against the British. He also helped to map some of Kentucky's earliest settlements, to write the documents upon which its government was founded, to guide the state into being, and then to hold it together during its first shaky years of existence.

His father was General Evan Shelby, who laid out the old Pennsylvania Road across the Alleghenies and distinguished himself by his gallantry in action in Indian campaigns that helped bring peace to the frontier and open the lands to settlement.

The Shelby family had come from Wales to make their home in Maryland, and that was where Isaac was born in 1750. He learned to fish and hunt, to track game through the forest and to use a gun, before he could read or write. As a boy, he worked on his father's farm, helped neighbors clear their lands, and developed skill as a surveyor. He was hardly out of his teens when he served the area as a deputy sheriff.

Isaac was a sturdy youth, medium tall, with a prominent nose, clear deep-set eyes, and a face reddened by sun and wind. He was proud of his strength and of being able to work harder than most boys his age. When Isaac was in his early twenties, the Shelby family moved across the Alleghenies to make a new home in western Virginia. For a time, he was what a later age called a cowboy, herding and managing cattle while his father followed a military career.

The Indian raids that were terrorizing settlers brought him to his father's side. Isaac served as a lieutenant in his father's company in a decisive frontier battle at the mouth of the Kenhawa River. It was fought from dawn to sunset for half a mile along the riverbank and when other officers were killed by Indian arrows, the Shelbys took command. They finally routed the Indians in a historic victory.

Virginia ordered a fort built on the ground where the battle was fought and Isaac was named second in charge of the garrison. He served there until the post was disbanded in July 1775 when Virginia's royal governor became afraid that patriot rebels might capture the fort and turn it to use against the Crown.

Richard Henderson and the Transylvania Company were opening up the new lands of Kentucky to settlement and Shelby went to work for them as a surveyor. For more than a year, he lived in the wilderness, breaking trails and mapping paths through the forests, laying out some of the first sites the land speculators sold.

Sleeping in the open in all kinds of weather, he often was without bread, salt or proper food. With his own ox he helped to clear the way for homes, not guessing then that he someday would help bring the settlement to statehood. He also looked for a place to build a future home of his own and started laying out the tract and improving it.

While he was away from Virginia, the full storm of revolution broke. Shelby returned to find that the Committee of Safety had named him to captain a company of minutemen.

Governor Patrick Henry soon put him in charge of furnishing supplies for the patriot troops stationed at various garrisons to guard the frontier settlements.

Shelby was still busy organizing the vital supply lines, some of which stretched out for more than three hundred miles, when he also was chosen to help make a treaty with the Cherokee Indians.

In 1778 he helped to furnish supplies for the Continental Army and for an expedition against the Detroit and Ohio Indians. The following year, he provided boats for the campaign against the Chicamauguas. He used his own personal credit to get needed goods for the pocket-poor troops.

That spring, Shelby was elected a member of the Virginia legislature from Washington County. In the fall Governor Jefferson made him a major of the guards who escorted a party of commissioners to fix the new boundary line between Virginia and North Carolina. When the line was extended, Shelby found that his previous Virginia home had been put within the limits of North Carolina. He promptly was made a North Carolina colonel.

But with all his activities, he was anxious to return to the future homesite he had begun to lay out for himself in Kentucky. He went back to finish clearing the land in the summer of 1780, but hardly had time to look around before he was called upon to help check the British forces which had overrun two Southern states and were on the border of North Carolina.

The Revolutionary armies were suffering serious defeat. There was panic and the men in the militia began to quit and return to their homes. Shelby suggested to the other officers that they raise an army of volunteers from among the backwoodsmen and surprise the British by continuing the attack instead of making an expected retreat.

He led the raw, undisciplined riflemen against the superior British army. They served without any authority from the government under which they lived, without pay, rations, supplies or even enough ammunition, and with little hope of success. But at King's Mountain they won a victory which helped turn the tide of war in the South. They killed the British general and several hundred of his officers and men, captured hundreds more, and caused such disaster that Cornwallis ordered the disorganized retreat of the main British army.

The North Carolina legislature voted its thanks to Shelby. He was elected a member of it in 1782, but he returned to Kentucky the following spring. There he married Susanna Hart, daughter of one of the proprietors of the old Transylvania Company, and at last began to build his home. With the end of the war, the real flood of settlement began and Shelby soon was looked to for leadership in the campaign for independent statehood.

He was named chairman of the first convention held in Danville in 1784 to consider the question of parting from Virginia. Each militia company in Kentucky had elected one delegate. The issue was gravely debated, with a majority in favor of separation, but Shelby and the others decided the military men should not act on their own. A second and then a third convention was called, with delegates chosen by vote of all the settlers.

Finally a strong petition was drawn up and sent to the Virginia assembly, which promptly agreed to the separation under certain conditions. The most important of these was that the Federal Congress should, in advance, consent to the admission of Kentucky into the Union. Many Kentuckians resented that. They wanted independence for Kentucky, but didn't want to be forced to join the Union.

There were those who demanded immediate and unconditional separation even if it meant war against Virginia. Others wanted to hold to the ties with the mother state. Some called for an independent Kentucky republic. General James Wilkinson, a wily and ambitious plotter who hoped to set up a personal empire in the new West, urged Kentucky to ally itself with Spain, which controlled trade down the Mississippi and the port of New Orleans.

Shelby held out for moderate action. One Danville convention followed another, each putting forth the call for the next one or being summoned to meet by the Virginia assembly. But it wasn't until the third act for separation had been passed by Virginia and the seventh convention had met in Kentucky that the parting finally came, after six years of political wrangling.

Congress passed an act that would admit Kentucky to the Union June 1, 1792. Shelby was appointed by Congress to a board of war to defend the new frontier state against the Indians. In April he took part in the convention that framed the state constitution along the general lines of the Federal Constitution. Twenty-four days after Kentucky became a state, he was elected its governor.

He had no easy task holding the new state together. It still festered with violent disputes and differences. There was constant trouble with the Indians and anger against the weak Federal Government for not giving settlers enough protection from Indian raids. Officers of the state militia were at odds with those of the national army. In addition, Shelby also had to deal with a touchy international problem.

The French ambassador to the United States, revolutionary Edmond Genêt, tried to organize a band of Kentuckians to fight Spain at New Orleans. Louisiana was under Spanish control and Spain was a major enemy of France. Genêt gained a strong following in Kentucky, where many sympathizers saw in the plan a way to end Spain's domination over the Mississippi River trade.

Shelby had to steer a careful course so as not to side with the Federal Government against his own state. But when General Washington appealed to him to halt the threat of a Kentucky-based war against Spain, he acted to stop the mass invasion.

When his four years as governor were over, Shelby turned down re-election. He retired to private life, devoted himself to his home, to business activities, and to raising his family of thirteen children. He took no direct part in politics for eighteen years.

But in 1812 another war with Britain brought him from retirement to answer the call of his people for leadership. Once more he was elected governor. Although then an aging man of sixty-two, he raised a force of four thousand Kentucky volunteers and led them in person to join with General Harrison in an invasion of Canada. This brought the decisive defeat of the British at the Battle of the Thames, one of the few American land victories of the War of 1812.

Shelby declined the office of Secretary of War five years later. His last public act was serving with Andrew Jackson on a commission to buy the remaining lands of the Chicksaw Indians in Kentucky and Tennessee. He retired once again to his Kentucky home, Traveler's Rest, where he died in his seventy-sixth year, in 1826.

The whole nation honored him and Kentucky erected a monument over his grave. Counties in nine different states were named after him.

TENNESSEE

Motto: Agriculture, Commerce

Flower: Iris

Bird: Mockingbird

Tree: Tulip Poplar

Admitted to the Union: 1796

☆

Hernando de Soto, the Spanish explorer who led his men into the wilderness of the New World on a search for gold, traveled the mountainous area of what is now Tennessee in 1540. Nearly 150 years later, followers of French explorer Robert La Salle built a fort near what has become the city of Memphis.

The French claimed the land as part of Louisiana, but they lost their claims when the British won the French and Indian War. By treaty, the lands were granted to the Indians. However, mountain men and pioneer settlers from other colonies began moving in and making homes.

Men from Virginia brought their families to the Watauga River Valley in 1769. They and others who joined them there made the first attempt to set up a separate government. In 1772 they formed the Watauga Association.

North Carolina then created Washington County to make the settlements part of its state government. Later, after the troubles of the Revolutionary War and constant Indian attacks, North Carolina offered to turn the lands over to the United States to become federal property.

Settlers took it on their own to make a separate and independent state. They called it the State of Franklin. But the Federal Government finally organized the area as the Southwest Territory. Tennessee was created from the national territory and admitted to the Union as a state in 1796.

JOHN SEVIER

(*1745–1815*)

While he was still in his teens, John Sevier built a town out of the wilderness. When he became a man, he built a state.

Sevier was a cavalier in moccasins and buckskin. Born in Virginia's Shenandoah Valley in 1745, he grew up on the frontier to which his parents had come from England to make their home. He was nineteen when he planned and laid out the town of New Market, Virginia. He set up its government and ran its affairs.

While he was still a young man, he moved his family over the mountains to what is now eastern Tennessee. For more than forty years he was a leader of the men who created statehood, but he was far from being a typical politician.

Sevier was a hunter and explorer, a celebrated Indian fighter, a brave Revolutionary War general. He was bold, fiery, hard-muscled, swift in body and mind, a battling patriot whose life was dedicated to the right of men to govern themselves.

He led the first Watauga government until the area was taken under the protection of North Carolina. Later, when North Carolina wanted to rid itself of the responsibility and turn the land over to the Federal Government, Sevier became governor of the state of Franklin.

It was first called Frankland, or Land of the Free. Sevier and his neighbors voted to create a state of their own because they felt their rights were not being protected by North Carolina.

Delegates agreed to a constitution for their self-made state in 1785. They set up their own courts, judges, legislative body and full government. Sevier's yearly salary as governor was two hundred mink skins.

North Carolina refused to recognize Sevier's state. It maintained its own court and offices in a town ten miles from him.

The area had two sets of officials and rival sheriffs who constantly battled with each other. Frequently, they raided each other's offices to seize court records.

Frankland appealed to Congress in Washington to accept it into the Union as a separate state, but the plea was turned down. Sevier then wrote to Benjamin Franklin, seeking his help, and offering to change the name of the state to Franklin in his honor. The old philosopher thanked him for the compliment, but advised the state of Franklin to make peace with North Carolina.

During the four years that the state of Franklin existed, Sevier waged a personal war to keep it going. Once, when he returned home from battling Indians who threatened the settlers, he found that his estate had been raided and his property had been seized and carried off by the legal agents of North Carolina.

With a body of troops and a small cannon, he marched on the home of John Tipton, leader of the North Carolina group. He beseiged the house, threatened to blast it apart, and fired warning shots into it. The small war lasted several days. It finally broke up when Tipton's men gathered a larger force and scattered the attackers.

The governor of North Carolina accused Sevier of treason as the self-styled governor of Franklin and ordered his arrest. Sevier was visiting an inn run by a Widow Brown one early morning when Tipton's men caught up with him. The widow, a heavily built woman, tried to save him.

She pulled a rocking chair into the narrow doorway of her inn, plumped herself down into it, and calmly refused to move. The North Carolina agents threatened and blustered, but they couldn't budge the widow or get past her rocking chair.

However, Sevier gave himself up to the agents, to keep his own followers from becoming involved in what he feared might be a deadly riot. Handcuffed, he was led over the mountains toward a jail in Morgantown, North Carolina.

On the way, Sevier was warned of a plot to murder him. His guards intended to let him break free and then to shoot him for attempting to escape. When he refused to fall into the trap, one of the guards shot at him anyhow, but missed.

When Sevier was delivered to the jail in Morgantown, the sheriff there wouldn't lock him up. He took the handcuffs from Sevier's wrists and set him free at once.

Meanwhile, friends put up bond for his release. He had so many friends and followers armed with rifles that the North Carolina agents let him go. There never was any other attempt to try him for treason.

But the state of Franklin gradually began to lose power. The North Carolina assembly passed an act pardoning everybody who had been associated with the self-made state except John Sevier. The act declared that he was to be kept forever from "the enjoyment of any office of profit or honor or trust in the State of North Carolina."

His neighbors defiantly elected Sevier to the North Carolina state senate at the very next election. He waited outside the assembly building until the legislators lifted the ban against his holding office. They finally voted him his senate chair by a large majority.

His great popularity led to his election as governor of Tennessee when it was admitted to the Union in 1796. Sevier served three terms as governor, the limit allowed to any one man under the state constitution. He then went on to serve his new state for several terms in Congress, where he became a leader of the patriot cause in the War of 1812.

John Sevier died at the age of seventy in 1815, still an active man to the last. He was stricken with a fatal fever while on a trip to investigate claims to set the boundaries of Indian lands.

OHIO

Motto: With God, All Things Are Possible

Flower: Scarlet Carnation   Bird: Cardinal

Tree: Ohio Buckeye

Admitted to the Union: 1803

☆

Ohio was the first state to be formed from the famed Northwest Territory. Control of the land had long been disputed by the French and English, and before them by various Indian nations as well.

In 1749 the region was claimed for the French. At almost the same time, the Ohio Company was formed to extend the English settlements of Virginia to the west. The French claim was threatened by the Ohio Company's activities in surveying the river valley and encouraging colonists to settle. That was one of the causes of the French and Indian War. At the end of the war the land was given by treaty to the British.

However, the Indians rose against the British, and Britain decided that the territory could be governed better from Canada. The region was made part of Quebec in 1774, but the fact that several colonies held land claims there added to the discontent that led to the American Revolution.

When the land passed to the new United States after the Revolution, the confusing claims of several states had to be settled. That was done by all the states ceding almost all their western lands to the national government.

Settlers swarmed into the area almost as soon as the Revolution ended. Land booms and failures, even Indian raids, slowed the Western movement only slightly. After Anthony Wayne routed organized Indian resistance at the Battle of

Fallen Timbers in 1794, an even greater number of families moved west.

Five years later, the Northwest Territory was reduced to about the size of Ohio, with a government separate from the rest of the territory. In another four years Ohio became a state.

THOMAS WORTHINGTON
(1773–1825)

Thomas Worthington was twenty-three when he first saw the Ohio lands. Although he had seen many other parts of the world in his young life, no place had ever looked so good to him. It was nearly two years before he could move there. For more than a quarter of a century after that, he helped to build Ohio. The state made him rich and left him poor, but he never faltered in his love for the new land, and Ohio never ceased to honor him.

Worthington was born in Charleston, Virginia (now West Virginia), three years before the Declaration of Independence. His father died when he was very young and he was brought up by his older brothers. In 1791, shipping on a Scots merchant vessel, he set out to see the world. After two years at sea, he was quite happy to return to his Virginia home and decided to make surveying his career.

His work took him to Ohio in 1796 and he soon was telling friends back home about the opportunities he saw there for a man to make himself a rich future. Worthington encouraged some of his friends to join him in buying land near Chillicothe that had been set aside by Virginia for purchase by Revolutionary War veterans.

That December, he married Eleanor Van Swearingen and they spent the first year and a half of their marriage severing ties with Virginia, freeing their slaves, and making plans to move to Ohio. When they did in the spring of 1798, Worthington's brother-in-law, Edward Tiffin, went with them. Although young Worthington was not wealthy, he had enough money when combined with part of his wife's inheritance to enable him to live the life of a country gentleman and to invest in some nearby mills.

As was to be expected of a man who had left the old lands of Virginia for the new freedom of the West, he was quick to join the ranks of the new Jeffersonian Republicans. Within months, his neighbors looked to him for leadership and elected him to represent them. He was a member of the territorial house of representatives from the time it was established in 1799 until Ohio became a state.

The territory then included not only what is the present state of Ohio, but also half of what has become the eastern peninsula of Michigan. It was a vast area over which the Federalist Party governor, old and aristocratic Arthur St. Clair, had enormous power.

St. Clair and those who supported him wanted to keep the control of the Ohio Territory. Young Worthington and other Virginians who had settled near Chillicothe were anxious to remove St. Clair as a symbol of old-style government and to form a state.

The St. Clair group tried to have the territorial boundary lines changed so as to keep themselves in power. While they did not openly oppose statehood, they suggested plans that were sure to fail, so that no state would be created. They tried to put Chillicothe outside the limits of the province, to move the capital from there to Cincinnati, and to put through other political schemes.

St. Clair ruled almost as a dictator. His Federalists had a majority in the territorial legislature. But those who wanted a state had not moved to a new land merely to submit to what they considered Federalist tyranny. Feelings ran so high that a riotous mob opposed to St. Clair's one-man rule stormed the governor's house and nearly succeeded in dragging him out to the street. Worthington was one of the few who kept a calm head. Realizing that violence would defeat everything they were working for, by turning public sympathy against them, he stepped before the mob. Quietly, forcefully, arguing reason instead of emotion, he managed to talk the mob out of its angry mood.

The men of Chillicothe realized they had very little chance of establishing statehood through the legislature that remained under St. Clair's control. They decided to send Worthington to Washington to explain the situation to President Jefferson, members of Congress and other leaders.

In Washington, Worthington did his job well. He was an impressive man, six feet tall and sandy-haired, with a ruddy outdoor look about him that commanded attention. He found eager listeners among the Jeffersonians for his proposal for a strong western state. They wanted a new state that would be solidly on their side.

The House of Representatives overwhelmingly turned down the Federalist proposals endorsed by St. Clair. Instead, on April 30, 1802, the House passed the enabling act which permitted the territory to hold a convention to decide whether to establish a state and, if the decision was in favor of it, to form a constitution.

Jubilant over the victory, Worthington returned to Ohio to prepare for the difficult campaign to elect delegates to the convention. The St. Clair Federalists bitterly fought the whole idea of such a convention. They argued that the region still did not have enough population to decide about statehood. They tried to convince voters that a territorial government was cheaper and a state government would mean higher taxes.

When the issue was put to the people themselves, however, the vote was for delegates who wanted a state and an end to St. Clair's rule. The convention quickly voted for statehood. Within weeks, the same delegates framed a constitution for the new state of Ohio.

Thomas Worthington ran for United States Senator in the first election and won easily. In Washington he gained a reputation as an authority on public lands and frontier affairs. Elected to a second term, he voted against the declaration of war with Britain in 1812 because he felt the country was not prepared for it and also because he was a devoutly religious man with conscientious objections to war.

He resigned from the Senate in 1814 after he had been elected governor of Ohio, to succeed his brother-in-law, Edward Tiffin, the state's first governor. Under the Ohio constitution, the governor had been given almost no power. The people, so long under St. Clair's rule, had been afraid of creating another powerful executive.

Although Worthington could not command action, or dictate it as St. Clair had, he did use his position as governor to suggest it. Once again, by reasoning rather than by force, he offered ideas that brought many regulations and reforms helpful to the state. Even when he retired after his second term as governor, he promoted better farming methods, proposed state-supported schools, and supported the Ohio canal system to help increase trade.

His personal fortune took a downward turn after the depression of 1819. He had given so much of his time to the making of his state that some of his own business had been neglected. Finally, he was forced to sell his beloved home and lands. Until two years before his death at the age of fifty-two, however, he still served Ohio as a member of the state house of representatives. Even with his own land gone, he kept his love for the land he brought to statehood.

LOUISIANA

Motto: Union, Justice, Confidence
Flower: Magnolia Grandiflora   Bird: Brown Pelican
Admitted to the Union: 1812

Louisiana was the first non-English colony to be taken into the United States. Its residents had a culture, customs and language foreign to the rest of the country.

First visited by the Spanish, the area was claimed for France in 1682 and named in honor of Louis XIV. For nearly a hundred years, French settlers established their customs in the region. Then Spain took most of it from France by the terms of a secret treaty between the two governments.

The people of Louisiana revolted against the first Spanish governor and finally forced him to flee to Cuba. The next governor came with strong troops, threw the leaders of the revolt into prison, and enforced Spanish laws. The customs of Spain soon masked the earlier ones of France.

New Orleans aided the English colonies during the American Revolution and, after Spain openly entered the war against Britain, troops from Louisiana captured some nearby settlements. After the Revolution there was a long period of dispute over American rights to use the Mississippi River.

America made a treaty with Spain in 1795, but seven years later the navigation rights were taken away. The territory was returned by Spain to France, but in 1803 Napoleon unexpectedly sold the whole region to the United States.

WILLIAM CLAIBORNE
(1775–1817)

William Claiborne had the ill luck to be governor of two of the most troublesome territories of the United States. Both were melting pots of many conflicting nationalities at a time when America's culture was mostly English. Both were overrun with river pirates, swindlers, gamblers and other ruffians. Both had been involved in international plots of one kind or another.

That a man sent to bring order, law and respectability to such areas should even remain alive was remarkable. That he also should do a good job for the United States in the seventeen years of his service is testimony to the kind of a man William Claiborne was.

By the time he was fifteen, the Virginia-born lad had finished school at Richmond Academy, attended classes for awhile at William and Mary College, and was working in Washington for the clerk of Congress. In the halls of Congress, he heard the great orators of his day and he loved to imitate them. Tennessee's state maker, John Sevier, heard the boy and was impressed with his speech-making talent. He urged him to go back home to Virginia and study to be a lawyer.

Claiborne took the advice. When he completed his studies he set up a law office in Tennessee and soon gained local fame as a frontier criminal lawyer. Sevier helped him politically and Claiborne was chosen a delegate to the convention that made the constitution for the new state of Tennessee. After Sevier became governor, he named Claiborne a judge of the state supreme court.

Claiborne was elected to Congress in 1797 to fill out the term of Andrew Jackson, who had become a Senator. Although Claiborne was still several years younger than the established minimum age for Congressmen, he was re-elected to serve a full term.

Claiborne worked to win the support of Tennessee's voters for Jefferson in the presidential election, and in 1801 Jefferson named him governor of the Mississippi Territory. It was a position of high trust for a young man of twenty-six. Claiborne married his sweetheart, Elizabeth Lewis, and set out at once for Natchez.

He hardly realized the troubles he was walking into. During the previous century, the area had passed back and forth from French to Spanish to English rule without any regard for the wishes of the people. They were no happier over the fact that the United States had taken control. The discontent of the settlers had been deepened by the harsh dictates of the governor who held the job before Claiborne.

His first task was to try to bring peace to the warring political groups in the territory and to patch up their quarrels. He had to organize counties and a working territorial government and there were many complicated land claims to settle. Farsightedly, he also made plans for public schooling and public health.

The Mississippi Territory was closely tied to adjoining Spanish-controlled Louisiana and there was strong unrest among the people after the port of New Orleans was closed to American trade just before France resumed control of it. There was also the difficulty of great distance from the government in Washington.

Against all these odds, Claiborne governed with a skill that won Jefferson's approval. But the President's praise and the promise of an assignment of greater responsibility were dimmed by a personal tragedy that suddenly struck his own life. After less than four years of marriage, his young wife, Elizabeth, died.

Meanwhile, American representatives in France had accepted Louisiana for the United States in April 1803. It took several months for the surprising news that Napoleon had sold the land to reach the general public. Even Jefferson wasn't quite sure how much land had been acquired or what conditions existed in the French-Spanish area, but control of the Mississippi River was of vital importance and he acted swiftly to secure it.

He appointed Claiborne and General James Wilkinson as commissioners to accept the province from the local authorities. Wilkinson previously had been involved in Spanish intrigues over the use of the Mississippi. When the territory was divided at what is now the northern boundary of Louisiana State, Claiborne was named governor of what became Orleans Territory.

In New Orleans, Claiborne's job was even harder than it had been in Mississippi. There had been no American governor before him and he had to build a completely new government. Many people were openly against being under American control and some took the stand that the United States had no right to buy the territory.

Claiborne had no knowledge of the laws that had governed the French-Spanish colonials. He knew very little of their long-established traditions, customs and habits. He could speak neither Spanish nor French and many of those with whom he dealt could speak no English.

Added to all his other problems was the conspiracy of Aaron Burr to establish a new Western empire built around Louisiana. Claiborne became involved in it because General Wilkinson, sent to Louisiana with Claiborne, had been closely associated with Burr. At first Claiborne defended Wilkinson's actions, and when Wilkinson confessed that he actually had a part in Burr's conspiracy, a great deal of popular feeling turned against Claiborne as well.

However, he so clearly demonstrated his strict honesty and good intentions in governing them that the people of the area gradually accepted his leadership and finally came to support him loyally. Most of them backed Claiborne during the frequent political quarrels he had throughout his terms in office.

Claiborne was far from being an easygoing man. He fought for the things in which he believed and had no fear of speaking his mind frankly in disputes with his associates. One such open exchange of political insults resulted in a duel in which he was badly wounded.

When President Madison approved the annexation of West Florida in 1810, he appointed Claiborne to take possession of the district of Baton Rouge and to make it part of the territory of Louisiana. Two years later, at the outbreak of war with Britain, Claiborne was faced with trying to defend a border state already troubled with inner problems of its own.

It was seething with smugglers and pirates, outlaws of all kinds whose activities increased with the coming of war. There were agitators from Mexico trying to arouse sympathy for a Mexican revolt. And the greatest problem of all was the outright lack of interest by both the people and the legislature in approving measures for adequate defense. Most of them simply just didn't care. Louisiana had seen many governments come and go.

After the British invaded the territory, old political wounds were opened when New Orleans was successfully defended by Andrew Jackson. Jackson was a political enemy of John Sevier, Claiborne's old friend and adviser from Tennessee. Bitterly Jackson denounced Louisiana for failing to give him proper support in fighting the British.

Claiborne warmly defended his people and their actions. His years of service in the territory had brought him deep understanding of their ways. The people, in turn, had replaced their early resentment of Claiborne with deep affection.

As territorial governor, he helped lead Louisiana to full statehood, with its acceptance into the Union in 1812. He was elected the new state's first governor and served for four years. Then he was elected to the United States Senate, but died before he could take office.

Governor of two troublous territories, state maker of one of them, William Claiborne was only forty-two years of age when death took him.

INDIANA

Motto: The Crossroads of America

Flower: Peony   Bird: Cardinal

Tree: Tulip (Yellow Poplar)

Admitted to the Union: 1816

☆

There were a few trading posts in Indiana in the late 1600's, but the first permanent settlement was made by eight French families in 1735 near what became Vincennes. At the time of the Revolution, all of Indiana was united with Canada by the British in an attempt to keep the Mississippi Valley from falling into the hands of the rebellious colonies. When it came into American control after the daring exploits of George Rogers Clark, there was ceaseless warfare with the Indians.

Although the treaty of 1783 made the land part of the United States, and it was included in the Northwest Territory that was organized some four years later, not many settlers dared make homes there because of the Indian attacks. The Northwest Territory was divided in 1800 and Indiana Territory was created from its western part. Indiana then included what became Illinois, Wisconsin and much of Minnesota and Michigan. Later, Indiana was divided twice again, to reduce it to its present size.

What really made statehood possible in Indiana was subduing the Indians and finding peace with them so as to open the area to full settlement. It was not until after the end of the second war with the British that enough people moved in so that Indiana could be admitted to the Union as a state by a joint resolution of Congress in 1816.

WILLIAM HENRY HARRISON
(*1773–1841*)

William Henry Harrison was an Indian fighter who became President. He served in the White House for only one month before his death. The real achievement of his career was in helping to open the new West to settlement. In doing that, he guided Indiana from a terrorized wilderness to a place among the states.

Many people thought of him as a man who rose from a log cabin to the Presidency, but that was part of the political publicity that surrounded his later years. Actually he had a distinguished family background.

Harrison was born to one of the first families of Virginia in a manor house on the banks of the historic James River. One of his ancestors, as a colonel serving under Cromwell, signed the death warrant of a king. His father, Benjamin Harrison, was a member of the Continental Congress, a signer of the Declaration of Independence, and governor of Virginia.

Following his father's wishes, he started out to become a doctor after he graduated from Hampden-Sidney College at the age of seventeen. Harrison went to Philadelphia to study medicine and entered the College of Physicians and Surgeons there. When his father died a short time later, Harrison decided he did not really want to be a doctor.

He had read about the Indian troubles in the West and his mind was filled with the excitement and adventure of that area. Harrison decided to quit the study of medicine to serve his country as a soldier against the Indians.

Robert Morris, a co-signer of the Declaration of Independence with Harrison's father, had become the boy's guardian. Morris argued with him and tried to persuade him that he was throwing away his future for a boyish dream of glory in a remote, wild land where he would come to no good end.

Young Harrison wouldn't listen. He pleaded directly with

General Washington to let him join the army. Washington finally gave in and commissioned him an ensign.

Harrison left immediately for Fort Washington, now Cincinnati. He was still only eighteen when he began what was to be twenty years of frontier warfare. Within a year, he had risen to the rank of lieutenant and soon was chosen by General Anthony Wayne as an aide. At Wayne's side, Harrison distinguished himself in the victorious Indian campaigns that followed. He was promoted to captain and put in command of Fort Washington when Wayne departed.

However, the quiet routine of garrison life, after active warfare, began to bore him. Once again he sought something more exciting to do. From military affairs he turned to politics, and attracted the attention of those who were looking for a spokesman who would give the new territory a greater voice in the nation's government.

When he was twenty-six he resigned from the army and was elected the territory's first delegate to Congress. Instead of fighting Indians, he turned to fighting a lobby of land-grabbing speculators.

Harrison led a successful battle in Congress to change the territory's land grant system so actual settlers would benefit from the disposal of public lands. Although only a territorial delegate, he was made chairman of the Committee on Lands. The reforms he put through encouraged more rapid settlement of the whole Northwest Territory.

It has been said that if he had done nothing else, Harrison's land reforms alone would entitle him to credit as Indiana's state maker, because they helped increase the permanent population upon which statehood was founded. But as his territory's delegate, he also helped Congress work out the plans to divide the old Northwest Territory into the states which grew out of it.

When Indiana was made a separate territory, Harrison was appointed its first governor by President John Adams. There was no legislature to check him, no local newspapers to report what he did, and he was given a power equal to that of an old

Roman governor over all the vast country lying between the then new state of Ohio and the Rocky Mountains.

If he had been a self-seeking young man or a greedy one, Harrison might have gained from many tempting offers by groups of speculators who wanted him to join in their land-grab schemes. Instead, he gained a reputation for honesty that was rare in the get-rich-quick days of the frontier. He might have ruled the wilderness domain as a despot, but he won his way to national leadership by the popularity he achieved for his temperate administration of Indiana.

When he took office the whole territory consisted of three main settlements, so widely separated it was impossible for them to join ranks in common defense against the Indians, who were often inspired in their raids by British agents and antigovernment traders. Harrison tried to deal peaceably with the Indians, promoted laws to give them better treatment, and concluded fifteen treaties to purchase title to upwards of seventy million acres of land for the United States.

By skilled and bold diplomacy the Indian fighter who had become governor managed for a decade to keep his old enemies from a general uprising, while more and more settlers came into the territory. Many of the Indian chiefs had learned to have faith in his character as a man who tried to keep his promises to them.

However, there arose among the Indians a religious leader who became known as the Prophet. He and his warrior brother, Tecumseh, hoped to combine all the tribes between the Ohio and the Great Lakes to keep settlers from taking more lands. They aroused their Indian followers to a passion by spreading the prophecy that the Indians were fated to destroy the intruders and rule supreme.

British agents encouraged them as war with the United States approached. Harrison tried to talk to the chiefs, but the trouble reached a crisis. He finally gathered a band of frontiersmen to support the militia and marched toward the Prophet's town at Tippecanoe. The whole frontier of the great Middle West was at stake.

The Indians, under British direction, attacked. In what

sometimes is considered the opening skirmish of the War of 1812, Harrison won a victory over the Indians and became a national hero. He went on to command the forces that drove the Indians and British into Canada, where Tecumseh was slain. The Middle West was freed of the ambitions of the British and the dread of the Indians.

On a visit to the East, people in New York, Philadelphia and Baltimore wildly cheered him, and his great popularity later led him to the Presidency. Meanwhile Indiana, finally freed of Indian terror, grew in population with the war's end. More than sixty thousand settlers had moved in by the time it was admitted as a state in 1816.

MISSISSIPPI

Motto: By Valor and Arms

Flower: Magnolia Blossom   Bird: Mockingbird

Tree: Magnolia

Admitted to the Union: 1817

☆

Mississippi first was a region controlled by three powerful Indian tribes: the Choctaw, Chickasaw and Natchez. Explorer de Soto's men visited it in 1540, but no Europeans settled in the area until the French set up a small colony on Biloxi Bay in 1699.

It was a French colony until the English took it over at the end of the French and Indian War. For a brief period, English settlers poured into the region and established plantations that grew rice and indigo. During the American Revolution the territory was captured by Spain, and despite American treaty rights, Spain held control until nearly 1800.

After Georgia gave up its western lands, and following the Louisiana Purchase, there was a great land boom in Mississippi. Settlers from Southern and mid-Atlantic states as well as some from New England moved into the new territory along one of the most famous roadways in America, the Natchez Trace.

This road grew from early Indian trails and originally was a one-way street traveled by traders from western lands. They floated their merchandise down the Mississippi on rafts, and then, having sold everything including the lumber that made the rafts, returned by walking the Natchez Trace up to Nashville and points north. Because the returning merchants usually were carrying the money they had made, the Trace also became notorious for its robbers and thieves.

DAVID HOLMES
(1770–1832)

David Holmes guided Mississippi as a father might lead a child, through the fears and troubles of its early years into its growing up as a state. Since he remained a bachelor all his life, the state almost seemed to take the place of the family he never had.

He and his older brother, Hugh, were born in Pennsylvania where his father had settled after coming to the New World from the north of Ireland. In the years just before the Revolution, when the two boys still were very young, the family joined other Pennsylvania farmers who moved into Virginia's Shenandoah Valley.

David's father started a crossroads store in Winchester. When he finished school there at the age of fifteen, David went to work for his father, keeping the store books and becoming a partner in the business. But his brother was making a name for himself as a lawyer who soon would be a judge and, after five years of country storekeeping, David decided to give it up and follow his brother's example.

He went to Williamsburg to study law, was admitted to the bar, and opened a law office at Harrisonburg, some seventy-five miles south of his family's home. As a popular young man in the community, he entered politics and was chosen commonwealth attorney for Rockingham County. Four years later, he ran for Congress as a Jeffersonian Republican and won the election.

His career as a Washington lawmaker led to six terms in the House of Representatives before his fellow Virginian, President James Madison, appointed him governor of the territory of Mississippi. David Holmes took the job knowing little of what to expect in the rough and still-wild land he was to govern.

The territorial capital at Natchez was supposed to have become part of the United States under the treaty signed at the end of the Revolutionary War. Another treaty in 1795 definitely gave it to the United States. But actually the local Spanish officials refused to give it up until troops were sent in less than ten years before Holmes arrived.

Just how far the territory reached and where it ended was marked by uncertainty. The sparsely settled lands were menaced by tribes of hostile Creeks and somewhat less than friendly Choctaws. Because of the Indians, the new governor and other Americans in the Mississippi settlements were in constant danger of being cut off from the rest of the country.

South of Natchez, Spain still claimed a region also claimed by the United States. American settlers there were rebellious against the Spaniards who kept authority. They threatened revolt to throw off Spanish taxes and Spanish rule, just as they had fought in the Revolution against the oppressive taxes of the British.

There wasn't much chance that any revolt would succeed and it took strong persuasion by Holmes to keep the settlers from rising up in arms to battle for their freedom. Within the borders of the territory itself, anti-Spanish feeling also was running high because of customs duties Spain imposed on trade.

As governor, Holmes had to keep the feelings of the settlers in check so as not to upset the delicate balance of American diplomacy. He had to prevent the slightest action that might antagonize Spain, which was a friendly nation to the United States, even if the Americans in Mississippi weren't friendly toward the Spaniards nearby.

He also had to serve as the eyes and ears of the government far away in Washington, to provide the information upon which American policy could be planned. His knowledge of the people and of those who would be friendly to American interests paved the way for Governor Claiborne of Louisiana to occupy the district of Baton Rouge. That led, in turn, to Mississippi's later taking in the Mobile district as part of the territory.

Meanwhile the Creek Indians, who once had hated the Spanish and had welcomed first the British and then the Americans, turned against all white settlers as more and more Americans made homes in the Mississippi Territory. When the long-feared Indian war finally came, Holmes was ready for it. He dispatched troops at once and they scored a decisive victory that put down the Creeks.

It wasn't until after the War of 1812 that Holmes was able to guide the territory gradually through the changes that brought it to statehood. He supervised the signing over of two large tracts of land by the Choctaw and Chickasaw Indians. With peaceful conditions assured and the great new rush of settlers who came especially to the river and Gulf Coast areas after the war, he was able to urge the government to divide the territory into two sections that could be more easily governed.

The eastern part became the territory of Alabama and the western part asked to be accepted into the Union as the state of Mississippi. Holmes presided over the convention that framed the first state constitution. When Mississippi officially became a state on December 10, 1817, he served as its first governor.

Holmes decided not to run for governor in the next election and went instead to the United States Senate. He was re-elected a Senator and then resigned in 1825 after he was overwhelmingly returned to the governorship. However, a few months after he took office, ill health forced him to retire.

During his last years of service to Mississippi, he worked for a more liberal state constitution, which finally was put into effect in 1832. By then, David Holmes had returned to his first home town of Winchester, Virginia, and lived to the age of sixty-two near the place where he had started as a country storekeeper.

ILLINOIS

Motto: State Sovereignty, National Union

Flower: Butterfly Violet   Bird: Cardinal

Tree: Burr Oak

Admitted to the Union: 1818

French explorers and missionaries were the first to visit the primitive Indian lands that became Illinois. After the French and Indian War, the British took over from the French. When Americans gained control following the Revolution, the area was made part of Indiana Territory and then a separate territory in 1809.

Settlement was very slow until after the War of 1812. Despite the war and Indian attacks which led to a massacre near Fort Dearborn, settlers moved toward eventual statehood by choosing members of an assembly, adopting a territorial constitution and electing a representative to Congress.

The old boundary of the Northwest Territory was changed to include part of the curve of Lake Michigan when the region that was to become a state was set up. This the settlers wanted so that commerce could move to the north as well as to the south.

Fur trade still flourished over most of Illinois when it was admitted as one of the United States in 1818. But the hunters and trappers soon were crowded out by homesteaders coming down the Ohio by flatboat and barge and across the Genesee wagon road to build their log cabins and to clear the land for farms.

JESSE THOMAS

(*1777–1853*)

Jesse Burgess Thomas began two political careers before he
came to Illinois. Personal tragedy ended the first one and
drove him westward. His action in helping to create separate
government for Illinois made him start over a second time. In
his own life he followed the pattern of constant adventuring
toward new frontiers that was typical of the nation during the
years in which he lived.

Born in Virginia in 1777 of a family whose ancestors included Lord Baltimore, he made his first move toward the
West when he was still in his twenties by journeying to Washington, Kentucky, to study law with a brother who had
moved there. He opened a law office and entered politics as
a county clerk of Mason County.

An ambitious young man who captured the attention of
political leaders, he married and settled down to what might
have been a lifelong career of law and public office in Kentucky. But his wife's sudden death in 1803 grieved him so
deeply that he felt he no longer could bear to go on living in
the place where they so happily had made their home.

Throwing aside his promising career, he moved farther west
in his search for a new life. By 1805 he was practicing law at
Lawrenceburg in Indiana Territory. He was elected to the
lower branch of the territorial legislature and appointed captain of the Dearborn County militia by Governor William
Harrison.

In Lawrenceburg he met a widow, Rebecca Hamtranck,
whose husband had died the same year Jesse lost his wife.
Until they met, Rebecca, grieving over the loss of her husband
just as Jesse Thomas had over the death of his wife, had
despaired of finding future happiness. Brought together by
Governor Harrison, who had become guardian of Rebecca's

young son, they fell in love and were married just before Christmas in 1806.

His future bright again, Jesse Thomas ran for election as an Indiana territorial representative and was sent to Washington in 1808. Most of the votes that put him in office came from settlers who lived in the western lands of the territory. He served them in Congress by presenting the bill to create the new territory of Illinois. It was passed before the end of his first session in Washington.

By the act itself, he cut away from Indiana the voters who had supported him. With his success in creating Illinois, he realized that the service he had "rendered the Illinoisians was fatal to further political aspirations in Indiana." He asked President Madison to appoint him as one of the three federal judges of the new Illinois territory, and the President agreed.

During the nine years he served as judge, he gained a reputation for fairness and shrewd ability at a time when Illinois was plagued with petty and quarrelsome disputes over old land claims. It was also a period of population boom, when the area swelled with new homesteaders.

When a constitutional convention was called in 1818, Jesse Thomas was the elected delegate from St. Claire County. The other delegates chose him to serve as the convention president. Thus he became not only the man who had won from Congress the creation of the territory, but also the leader who helped bring Illinois into being as a state.

In the elections that followed, Thomas was voted one of the first two United States Senators the new state sent to Washington. Among the bills he presented was one that amended the Missouri Compromise to set the boundary limits of slavery, but most of his lawmaking was devoted to the interests of his state rather than to national affairs.

After two terms as Senator, he decided not to run again for office. Retiring from Illinois politics, Thomas moved to Mount Vernon, Ohio, with his wife, who owned some property there. Although it was quite small, he managed it so as to start them on their way toward a modest fortune.

In 1840 Jesse Thomas had the honor of nominating William Harrison, his stepson's guardian and by then an Ohio neighbor, as candidate for President. Thomas was sixty-three years old and it was his last important act on the national political scene, although he lived for another thirteen years.

He and his wife Rebecca enjoyed forty-five years of happy married life before she died three years prior to his own death in 1853.

ALABAMA

Motto: We Dare Defend Our Rights

Flower: Camellia

Bird: Yellowhammer

Tree: Longleaf Pine

Admitted to the Union: 1819

When the land from the Mississippi River to the border of Georgia was organized as the Mississippi Territory in 1798, after having been under both English and Spanish rule, it was still mostly a wilderness. In only about twenty years, Alabama grew out of it to be one of the United States. Cotton brought the change.

The growing of cotton had just begun when it was interrupted by the War of 1812, which also slowed the lively fur trade. During the war the Creek Indians were aroused by the British to massacre settlers. The defeat of the Indians by Andrew Jackson brought peace to the area and opened the way for the real cotton growing boom.

English mills needed cotton and the demand boosted prices high. Fertile land could be bought cheaply in the Alabama region, and hundreds of new settlers flooded in from neighboring states, especially from Georgia. Wealthy newcomers took up the rich bottomlands and established the great plantations that produced cotton for the Southern ports. Poorer settlers followed to farm the uplands.

Within only a few years, so many settlers came that the territory of Alabama was set up in 1817 as a needed government. In two years more, it was a state.

WILLIAM BIBB

(1781–1820)

William Wyatt Bibb was a doctor by profession and a Georgian by birth. He lived in Alabama for only three years of his very short life. But during that time, his guidance helped create the state.

Born in Amelia County, Georgia, Bibb was just starting school as a boy of seven when the new United States was formed under the Constitution. His grandfather had come from Wales to settle in Virginia and his father had been a captain in the Continental Army. Bibb's mother was related to Martha Custis Washington.

Even as a schoolboy, William Bibb wanted to be a doctor. When he was old enough, his family sent him to study at the University of Pennsylvania. Philadelphia was then the federal capital and he began to take an interest in the political happenings there.

When he graduated at the age of twenty, he hurried home to start his practice as a doctor at Petersburg, Georgia. Treating his patients for their bodily ills, he also listened to their other problems. Much of the talk he heard at home was about politics, as it had been in Philadelphia.

Bibb gradually became as much concerned with the ailments of government as with those described in his books of medicine. He finally let himself be persuaded to run for the Georgia House of Representatives. Bibb won the election and stood the next time as a successful candidate for the state senate.

While he was dividing his time between his medical practice and his duties as a state lawmaker, he met Mary Freeman, whose loveliness made others speak of her as "the Beauty of Broad River." They were married in 1803. Two years later, when he was barely old enough to qualify, he was elected United States Representative from his Congressional district.

He served in the house until 1813 and then was elected a Senator from Georgia. The pay that Senators received in those days was a small amount, based on the number of days they were in the Senate each year. When they decided to pay themselves an annual salary of $1,800, there was a storm of public protest.

Bibb resigned from the Senate and felt no inclination to seek votes again from a public that complained it was overpaying him. Although he was just thirty-two years old, he retired from public life to live with his family in Georgia.

However, when Alabama was set up as a territory in 1817, President Madison named him to become governor of it. There were some who openly asked how he qualified to be chief executive of the newly formed territory between Georgia and the new state of Mississippi. But the choice proved a wise one.

Bibb was experienced in both state and federal government, familiar with the region, and respected there. He had no strong ties with any of the leaders of the quarreling political groups in the area and he was a handsome young man with a beautiful wife who could help him make the friendships important to his success.

William and Mary Bibb moved immediately to St. Stephens, Alabama, where he set about establishing the basis of government and advising the people how to move toward statehood. It was a giant step for them to take from frontier life to equal status with the other states. That Alabama was able to take it in just under two years has been credited largely to Bibb's guidance.

He helped Alabama form an efficient legislature, advised the people in making their constitution, showed them the way to achieve the state government for which they were so eager. When the constitution was accepted, Bibb was continued in office as governor by popular vote.

A year later, he was horseback riding one day when a storm broke suddenly. Frightened by the thunder and lightning, his horse threw him. Bibb was carried to his home, where he died a short time later. He was only thirty-nine years old.

MAINE

Motto: I Guide

Flower: Pine Cone and Tassel   Bird: Chickadee

Tree: Eastern White Pine

Admitted to the Union: 1820

☆

Maine was a reluctant part of Massachusetts for years before it broke away and became a separate state. Almost from the time the English colonies were founded in America, there were disputes over whether Maine belonged under the control of Massachusetts.

During the French and Indian War and again during the Revolution, many of Maine's settlers felt dissatisfied. The feeling was deepened by the natural differences between the people of aristocratic Boston and the rugged, simple farmers to the north. As early as 1785, a convention was called to discuss formal separation from Massachusetts.

But it was the War of 1812 that really brought sharp conflict, when the region felt that the Boston government had not done all it should have done to defend it. In the years immediately after the war, the demand for a break with Massachusetts grew to a full bid for independent statehood.

Maine was ready to become a state in 1819, but its formal entry into the Union was delayed nearly a year because it would have upset the even balance between free and slave states. Finally, in 1820, Maine was paired with Missouri and both were admitted together as a result of the Missouri Compromise that avoided a showdown, for a time, over the question of slavery.

WILLIAM KING
(1768–1852)

William King was born at Scarboro, Maine, only thirteen years after his half brother, Rufus King, famed statesman of the Constitution. But William's childhood was so completely different they might have been born of separate families.

Their father, Richard King, was a wealthy lumber exporter, but his wealth was built upon his own active knowledge of the business and the world markets. When he died, his estate dwindled away and there was no legacy to educate William in the same fashion as the older sons.

Rufus had been given a Harvard education, training in the law, and the background of a polished gentleman who became a Federalist leader and his party's candidate for President. He was already on his way toward fame when William was born as the seventh child of his father's second marriage. At the time of their father's death, William was just seven years old. He was given very little formal education and had to go to work as a laborer in Maine's sawmills at the age of thirteen.

Carefully saving his small earnings, he finally was able to start a successful business partnership with a brother-in-law. William was thirty-two years old before he began a career of his own. He moved then to Bath, where he lived the rest of his life, and by wise investment and keen business skill gradually built for himself the fortune he had failed to inherit.

Before many years more, William King was the proprietor of flourishing shipbuilding yards. He had his own ships, the first bank in Bath, a share in Maine's first cotton mill, and large real estate holdings. Even before he moved to Bath, he had entered politics, serving as a state representative. He was elected to represent his new home district of Bath and then was chosen a state senator.

During the War of 1812, he provided money and ships to help guard the coast of Maine. He was a major general of the state troops and a colonel in the United States Army. Although his shipping interests were hard hit by the war and he gave much of his time to public duty instead of to his own business, he came out of it a very wealthy and powerful man.

Residents nicknamed him "the Sultan of Bath." Some even accused him of having looked to his own interests by trading with the enemy. William King denied the charges. He wrote and published a pamphlet in which he defended his actions and hurled accusations of his own at the men who sought to prove he had been disloyal. The pamphlet helped to silence most of his accusers.

From the early days of the war, when King was organizing Maine's shore and inland defenses, he became angered over the lack of support given the area by Massachusetts, of which Maine was still a part. He began to stir up a one-man storm for Maine's independence and statehood.

He wrote letters by the score, circulated petitions, organized clubs that would work for separating Maine from Massachusetts, and arranged conventions. For seven years, during which time he held no important political office himself, he waged his campaign throughout the area, personally appealing to everyone who might have any influence on public opinion.

More than ever before, he felt his own lack of education. His opponents, who often couldn't find any logical answer to his common-sense arguments, made fun of his writings. They tried to discredit him as an ignorant clown by laughing at his unpolished literary style, the difficulty he had expressing himself in words, his poor grammar and the mistakes he made in spelling.

While the rude attacks hurt his pride, they couldn't stop him. He was strong with the confidence so many self-made men acquire. More than anything else, he wanted independence from Massachusetts. If there were those who laughed, there were others who would listen. And his rough, forceful, demanding arguments appealed to the common people who shared his feelings.

In 1818 he served for a year in the state senate again, to give an official sounding board to his pleas for what he thought was best for Maine. When the constitutional convention was called at last, in 1819, no one but William King was even considered for its presidency. He led the convention discussions, but there was very little to discuss. The people had waited for years to make their decision and, once it was made, they were eager for statehood.

But forces outside Maine had been at work and the Union was not ready to accept it as a state. The twenty-two states were in equal balance, slave and free. To admit Maine would give a majority to the antislavery forces in Congress. The political battle moved to Washington.

While Maine's sympathy was strongly against slavery, it also wanted to become a state. In the Senate, Rufus King denounced the Missouri Compromise as a cover-up and suggested there were better methods of dealing with the slavery problem. There were those who applauded the sentiments of William's famed half brother, but the stand he took delayed statehood for Maine.

Finally the Compromise went into effect. Paired with Missouri, Maine became a state. When the acceptance came, in 1820, there was no doubt in Maine as to whom the victory for statehood belonged. In the first election, the people chose William King their governor. Some twenty-two thousand votes were cast and all but a few hundred were for him.

He guided the state surely through the first year and set up its beginning government along lines that he hoped would give all political groups a voice in state affairs. The following year, he was called upon by the Federal Government to serve on a diplomatic mission involving Spain, and resigned as Maine's chief executive.

He was collector of customs for a time afterward, but he gradually lost his hold on local politics as the state grew and its outlook changed. Nationally, he was at odds with the principles of Andrew Jackson, whose wing of the Democratic Party rose to power. When King ran for governor again in 1835, he was overwhelmingly defeated.

He was then sixty-seven and he retired from active politics.

In his old age he was plagued by financial failures and family troubles. But "the Sultan of Bath" lived on to the age of eighty-four, a man whose iron-willed determination lifted him from the sawmills and the ignorance of his youth to the lasting respect of the state he helped bring into being.

PART III. SPREADING OUT THE NATION

MISSOURI

Motto: The Welfare of the People
Shall Be the Supreme Law

Flower: Hawthorn   Bird: Bluebird

Tree: Dogwood
Admitted to the Union: 1821

☆

When Missouri asked to be admitted to the Union as a slave state, there were many who were against allowing slavery in a new state so far north. Alabama, deep in the South, had been admitted and that had made the number of slave states exactly equal to the number of free states. One more state on either side would have given that side control of the United States Senate.

Northern Congressmen balked at letting Missouri enter unless it forbade slavery. Missourians resisted by taking a strong stand on the issue of States' rights. They argued that Congress had no right to forbid a new state any practices already permitted in any other state. Finally, in 1820, the Missouri Compromise was proposed. This forbade slavery in the rest of the area north of Missouri's southern border, but did not restrict it in the new state of Missouri itself.

For a while, Missouri's admittance was coupled with Maine's in the same bill, to maintain the exact balance of slave and free states. But the legality of this was questioned and finally two separate bills were prepared, one admitting Maine and the other enabling Missouri to form a constitution. However, statehood was still nearly a year away. It depended on a pledge to Congress by the Missouri legislature that nothing in the state constitution would abridge the rights of citizens of the United States.

ALEXANDER McNAIR
(1775–1826)

Alexander McNair was elected Missouri's first governor in August 1820. For almost a year he governed an unaccepted state whose first two Senators were left cooling their heels in the Capitol's corridors while waiting to take their seats. McNair led the support within Missouri for the amendments to the state constitution that were requested by Congress so that the state finally could be admitted to the Union in 1821.

The first governor of the state that became historically noted for compromise was himself something of a compromise. He was an American settler who married into one of the most aristocratic of the old French families of the area. It was these two factions, represented by McNair, which were able to break the hold that St. Louis politicians had on the territorial government.

Grandson of a Scotsman who had come to Pennsylvania nearly half a century before the American Revolution, Alexander McNair was born in 1775 on his father's farm in central Pennsylvania, northwest of Harrisburg. His father died when he was only two years old and his mother took him to a new home near Pittsburgh.

He grew up with very little education, joined the army as a youth, and then became an adventurer who decided to seek his fortune by striking out for the West. McNair arrived in

St. Louis in 1804 and the following March he married Marguerite Susanne de Reilhe.

Marguerite was beautiful, well educated and talented, the daughter of a prominent French merchant who had died three years earlier. Through his marriage, McNair was welcomed into the most influential business and political circles in the city.

As Americans pushed farther west, so did settlements in Missouri. St. Charles was a small post just a few miles west of St. Louis, across the Missouri River. It was considered "the last outpost of civilization" by growing numbers of westward pioneers who made it a supply point for the great overland journeys. Trade was booming there and McNair acquired real estate, businesses and other interests in the new community as well as in St. Louis. In 1809 when St. Charles was organized as a village, he was chosen one of the trustees. Later, during the first years of Missouri's statehood, St. Charles became the capital.

McNair's wide interests outside St. Louis gave him great influence with incoming settlers who mistrusted the well-organized city politicians. In addition to being a trustee of St. Charles, he held several other minor positions in the territorial government. As his personal popularity grew, he became the sheriff of St. Louis County, an officer and later inspector of the territorial militia, a U.S. Marshal, a Federal Indian agent, and the register of the St. Louis land office.

When he went as a delegate to the constitutional convention for the new state that was held in St. Louis in 1820, McNair wisely managed to keep from becoming involved in most of the political intrigue that was going on behind the scenes. But he won cheering approval when he spoke out against high salary schedules for state officials.

Before the convention was over, he announced that he would run for governor. His opponent, backed by the St. Louis politicians, was the extremely popular William Clark, of the famed explorer team of Lewis and Clark. McNair's chances of winning were considered slim.

During the campaign, the city politicians berated his lack

of education, claimed that he was an adventuring upstart who lacked ability, criticized his management of the land office, and tried to discredit him personally. But he had the quiet support of the conservative old families as well as that of the new settlers. Most of the attacks against him only pointed up how much like other new Western settlers he was. Voters who mistrusted the city politicians upset the election and chose him governor instead of Clark.

Missouri considered itself a state from the day it ratified its constitution, and McNair governed it without authority from Washington. Personally he was against any restrictions on slavery, but for the sake of achieving statehood without further delay, he urged approval of the amendment to the constitution that guaranteed the rights of citizens from other states within Missouri.

During the four years he was in office, McNair frequently called the legislature's attention to new laws in other states and urged that they be studied as possible models for Missouri. He retired after his one term as governor. Only two years later, on March 18, 1826, Alexander McNair died at the age of fifty-one.

ARKANSAS

Motto: The People Rule

Flower: Apple Blossom   Bird: Mockingbird

Tree: Shortleaf Pine

Admitted to the Union: 1836

☆

Arkansas first was visited by Spaniards led by Hernando de Soto in 1541. The French came more than a century later and established Arkansas Post for trading with the Indians. Under the French, the region became a part of the territory of Louisiana.

During the early eighteenth century, some settlers were brought in by a French colonization plan, but many of them left again when the movement failed. Arkansas remained almost entirely Indian country as the land passed from French to Spanish and then American control.

The cotton boom brought colonists from east of the Mississippi and treaties with the Indians opened more of the region to settlement. Arkansas County was established as part of the Missouri Territory in 1813 and the separate territory of Arkansas was created in 1819.

Much of the land was still undeveloped in 1836 when the constitutional convention met at the Baptist Church in Little Rock. On June 15th of that year, Arkansas was admitted as a state.

JAMES CONWAY

(1798–1855)

James Conway helped to lay out the boundaries and map the lands he later led into the Union as the state of Arkansas.

He came from a wealthy, slave-owning family and became owner of a vast cotton-growing plantation himself. He grew to leadership in an age of many financial scandals, when shrewd men plotted to use statehood as a means of gaining personal fortune.

Conway's grandfather was a prosperous Virginia planter who feared, during the Revolution, that the British would seize his property. He sent Conway's father into the western lands of Tennessee with his slaves and all movable property. After the Revolution the family settled there and young James Conway was trained as a surveyor.

He first came to Arkansas from Missouri in 1820 to help survey the public lands. Deciding that he wanted to make the area his future home, he bought a large tract along the Red River and built a cotton plantation that was worked by more than a hundred slaves. Named surveyor general of the territory, Conway held the office until Arkansas became a state.

Conway's surveying assignments took him from one end of the territory to the other. He took charge of marking out the western and southern boundaries and met many settlers as well as land speculators. Although his own cotton fields were far from the territorial capital at Little Rock, he began to take a deep interest in political affairs. Just before Christmas in 1826, he journeyed back to Tennessee to marry Mary Bradley and bring her home to his Red River plantation.

He was, by all standards, a very successful man and also a popular one. His friends were plantation owners like himself, wealthy and prosperous, and some of them saw in statehood a way to add to their private wealth. If Arkansas became a state, it would allow for the passage of banking laws that would let them reap high profits.

James Conway's motives were less selfish. Arkansas was his pride and he sought statehood for more patriotic reasons, but to some extent he was taken in by his friends, flattered by them when they chose him for their leader. There was very little direct political opposition. As the population boomed, the need for state government grew. Finally there were enough people to qualify Arkansas to become a state.

Delegates met quietly at the Baptist Church in Little Rock. James Conway and the others had no trouble in approving a constitution. He was asked to run for governor and won the office with little difficulty.

It was only then that his real troubles began. The new state needed money to finance its government. A group of men suggested opening two private banks whose finances were to be backed by issuing state bonds. The same plan had worked in other areas. Among the first acts passed by the new Arkansas legislature and signed by Governor Conway were those creating the banks.

Before long, Arkansas was seething with corruption and was over three million dollars in debt. The banks stopped making payments almost as soon as their doors were opened. They sent their own men to the legislature and influenced the courts.

His personal honesty unquestioned, Conway fought to hold together his new state, to save it from complete chaos. Newspapers of the day described the bankers as a "piratical crew," and Conway seemed powerless against them. But he did what he could to keep Arkansas from ruin. It was Conway's integrity and leadership that helped the state weather its financial storm.

When his term as governor was over, he was glad to retire and return to his Red River plantation. James Conway lived long enough to see his younger brother, Elias, elected governor of an administration that finally cleared up a good part of the state's debt.

MICHIGAN

Motto: If You Seek a Pleasant Peninsula, Look Around You
Flower: Apple Blossom   Bird: Robin (unofficial)
Admitted to the Union: 1837

Michigan was made part of Indiana during the first division of the old Northwest Territory, but became a separate territory in 1805. During the War of 1812, the British gained control of it until Commodore Perry's famous victory on Lake Erie returned most of it to the United States.

For more than a century before, Michigan had been a great uncharted wilderness. The area was the home of hostile Indians who kept out settlers. What maps there were showed the interior as a vast swampland.

Conditions changed after Lewis Cass became governor of the territory in 1813. During the eighteen years he served, the Indians were quieted, military roads were opened into the almost unknown land, settlements were encouraged and settlers were protected.

The territory's population rose from less than five thousand to more than thirty thousand by the time Cass left in 1831 to become Andrew Jackson's Secretary of War. With the growth of settlement, the territory molded from the wilderness began to clamor for statehood.

STEVENS THOMSON MASON

(*1811–1843*)

Born just a year before the outbreak of the War of 1812, Stevens Thomson Mason took control of Michigan's government while still in his teens.

He was typical of the young men of action who were to rise to power in the West. Although his extreme youth and inexperience later counted heavily against him, they served to his great advantage in the beginning.

The Masons were an old and respected Virginia family. Tom's father left Virginia before the boy was a year old and struck out for Kentucky to seek success as a lawyer. It didn't come easily and they moved from place to place throughout Tom's youth. For awhile, they lived as tenants on Henry Clay's estate.

A good student at school, Tom received high marks and qualified to enter Transylvania University. But by the time he was seventeen, he had to quit the university to take a job as a grocery clerk to earn money to help with the family's expenses.

His father, although hard-pressed by financial troubles, kept the friendship of men high in political office. In 1830, President Andrew Jackson appointed John Mason Secretary of Michigan Territory. Tom and his father packed immediately and set off together for the new frontier. They arrived in Detroit that July, but within a year, his father quit the job and left for Mexico.

John Mason told people he had private business to take care of in Mexico. His full reasons for resigning were never made clear. It might have been that John Mason decided on his own to seek his fortunes on still another frontier. There was talk, however, that he actually was sent to Mexico to take care of some personal business for President Jackson.

In any event, Jackson named young Tom to replace his father as Michigan's territorial secretary. Tom then was only nineteen. When, in the same month, Jackson called Michigan's beloved Governor Lewis Cass to Washington to be his Secretary of War, there were loud and indignant cries from the settlers that they were being "left to the mercy of infants and Indians."

President Jackson was not one to change his mind. He wanted a Secretary of War who was a good Indian fighter. Cass soon demonstrated his ability in conducting the Seminole and Black Hawk wars. Young Tom Mason, meanwhile, ignored the furor that his appointment created and set about showing people that he wasn't too young to manage the affairs of the territory.

Just a year and a week after his arrival in Michigan, he took the oath of office as territorial secretary. Modestly, and with good humor, he avoided political quarrels. Since he wrote very well, he carried on as much of the territory's business as he could by letter. He was also an excellent speaker. Soon he had people listening to the things he said and not just marveling that a boy could speak so well.

More and more, during the next five years, Tom took over the duties of the governor's office. He demonstrated a natural talent for political leadership. Not only was he able to get along well with most people, he also was able to bring together those of different views so as to work out compromises. When the question of statehood was first discussed, he took the lead in voicing a call for definite action.

He had been Michigan's chief executive in all but title, and in 1834 he was named governor of the territory. Tom used the office to pave the way for statehood. He called for a convention to meet early the following year. By May, the delegates had a constitution drawn up.

The constitution was approved by the voters at the election in October. At the same election, Stevens Thomson Mason realized his dream of becoming Michigan's first elected governor. He was twenty-four years old that month.

But there was another issue to be settled. The boundaries set for the proposed new state left out a section of land that was in dispute. Mason demanded return of this territory to

Michigan and sent state troops into Ohio to guard the disputed area. For nearly two years, he headed a Michigan government that was not included in the Union.

Finally the question of the disputed land was put before Congress. Although the decision was in Ohio's favor, Michigan received additional land. The entire Upper Peninsula, instead of only a small part of it, was included within Michigan's boundaries. Mason withdrew the state troops and Michigan was accepted, in 1837, as one of the United States.

During his two terms as governor, Mason showed active concern over public schooling, perhaps because his own chance to finish school had been cut short by lack of family funds when he was a boy. He appointed an excellent superintendent of public schools, used his veto power to protect university lands, and suggested many other laws and social reforms that were farsighted for the time in which he lived.

He knew very little about finance, however, and the state's treasury ran into serious money troubles because of his lack of experience in dealing with bankers. He was blamed for the difficulties and decided not to run again for the governorship. The legislature even refused to read his farewell message.

Rejected at twenty-nine by the state he had helped bring into being, Tom Mason went to New York to live with his wife and their three young children. He practiced law there for a short time before his death at the age of thirty-two.

In later years, romantic legends grew up around the story of the "boy governor." With the passing of time, many people felt he should not have been personally held responsible for financial mistakes shared by far more experienced men. In 1905 the body of Michigan's state maker was removed from New York and returned to Michigan to be buried with honor in Detroit's Capitol Square.

FLORIDA

Motto: In God We Trust

Flower: Orange Blossom   Bird: Mockingbird

Tree: Sabal Palm

Admitted to the Union: 1845

Florida's coast was known to early navigators and appears on some of the first maps of the New World. After some attempts by both the Spanish and the French to establish colonies, the first permanent Spanish settlement was begun at St. Augustine in 1565.

England took over Florida from Spain and settlers loyal to Britain flocked there during the American Revolution. The area remained loyal to the Crown and stayed mostly under British influence even when it was returned to Spain after the Revolution.

Pensacola served as a British base in the War of 1812, until Andrew Jackson captured the stronghold. Jackson, as temporary governor of the territory, accepted the transfer of it from Spain and stayed in Florida long enough to set up a beginning government.

A great rush of American settlement followed the opening of the territory until warfare broke out with the Seminole Indians. That held back more settlers for awhile, but the roads and maps made by the army during the Seminole War greatly aided Florida's later development.

Florida first applied for statehood in 1837. Although qualified, it was not admitted until 1845, when Iowa was paired with it to keep the balance of slave and free states.

RICHARD CALL

(*1791–1862*)

Born in Prince George County, Virginia, in 1791, Richard Keith Call was the son of a Revolutionary War soldier. He was named for an uncle who was a friend and aide to General Washington. When Richard was very young, his father died and his mother took him and three other children west to Kentucky.

He was needed to help support the family with his work in the fields, and there was little chance for him to go to school as a boy. It was not until he was nineteen, after his mother had died, that he was able to attend an academy in Tennessee for awhile. Most of his education was self-taught, just as in later life through his own studies he became a lawyer.

By the time he was in his early twenties, Call had put aside his books to be an Indian fighter. In 1813 he joined an expedition against the Creek Indians and later that same year volunteered to serve under General Andrew Jackson. He rose from the ranks to become a lieutenant.

When the whole company in which he served mutinied and threw down their arms to quit the army and leave for home, Call was the only officer who remained loyal and reported for duty as usual. General Jackson admired him for it and Call soon showed such daring courage in battle that the general formed a strong friendship for him.

He was commissioned a lieutenant in the regular army and served with Jackson's forces through the rest of the War of 1812, taking part in Jackson's great victory at New Orleans. By the time the war ended, Call was a captain and Jackson appointed him to his personal staff.

Under Jackson's command, Call had been with the troops that stormed Pensacola and wiped out the British base operating from the Spanish harbor. He negotiated the early peace terms there and three years later, in 1821, he prepared the way for Andrew Jackson to take over as temporary governor.

Call moved into Pensacola in advance of his old commander. While Jackson waited on the outskirts, fuming at the delay caused by the slow-acting Spanish officials, Call arranged the formalities for the transfer of Florida from Spain to the United States.

As soon as Florida officially was part of the United States, Call resigned his army commission and settled in Pensacola to practice law. Within two years he was a leader of the city government, was chosen a member of the first territorial council, and was appointed the territory's delegate to Congress.

Before he left for Washington, he married Mary Letitia Kirkham of Nashville, Tennessee. When he and his wife returned to Florida in 1824, they moved to Tallahassee, built a beautiful town house and then acquired a large plantation on the shore of Lake Jackson.

Call's old companion in arms, who by then was President Jackson, sent him to Havana to recover important title and land grant documents the Spaniards had taken with them when they left Florida. His study of the early Spanish surveys made him an expert in his law practice in dealing with disputes over land. Call frequently was consulted as an authority, and appeared before the Supreme Court to argue one of the land claim cases.

Jackson appointed him governor of Florida Territory in 1836 and Call lost no time in recommending statehood. It was at his official suggestion that the legislative council put the question before the voters the following year. The vote was in favor of becoming a state. On December 3, 1838, a convention met at St. Joseph and a constitution was adopted and signed in less than six weeks.

Florida had to wait more than six years before it was accepted as a state, because Congress wouldn't consider taking in a new slave state until there was also a new free state ready. During most of that time, until Iowa finally was accepted with Florida, Call was governor of Florida's territory-state.

Even before he was appointed governor, he had been

brigadier general of the Florida militia, active commander of the state troops fighting the Seminole Indians. During his first year as governor, he asked the War Department to grant him authority to conduct a summer campaign against the Seminoles. Despite his skill as an old-time Indian fighter and his careful military planning, the campaign failed and the War Department took away his command of the troops.

Call was furious. Angrily he denounced his military superiors in Washington. He accused them of injustice, of discriminating against him, of complete failure to understand the problems he had faced. He was so outspoken that President Van Buren removed him as governor of Florida in 1839.

Outraged by what he considered the President's unfair action, Call promptly changed his political party. He turned all his influence to support the opposition candidate, William Henry Harrison, for President. As soon as Harrison was elected to replace Van Buren, Call was reappointed Florida's governor.

Unfortunately he had made strong political enemies as well as friends. In Florida's first election after it became a state, Call was defeated for governor by a very small margin. Bitterly disappointed that he had been rejected by the voters of the state he helped bring into being, he retired from active politics. In 1856 he was offered the nomination for Vice-President of the United States, but refused it.

Although he had no desire to seek office again, he continued to use his considerable power and influence to strengthen Florida as a state. As a slaveholder, Call supported slavery, but also feared the breaking up of the Union over the slavery question. In the days before the Civil War, he tried in every way he could to keep Florida from seceding.

Once the decision was made, Call promptly offered his services to the state and to the Confederacy. He was a man of seventy when the Civil War began, and his final offer of military service was regretfully turned down. Death came to him the following year at his plantation home, after some forty years of leadership in which he freed, created, governed and tried to preserve his state of Florida.

IOWA

Motto: Our Liberties We Prize and Our Rights We Will Maintain
Flower: Wild Rose   Bird: Eastern Goldfinch
Admitted to the Union: 1846

☆

Iowa came to the United States as part of the Louisiana Purchase. Lewis and Clark traveled through it in 1804 and Zebulon Pike and later American explorers also mapped the region. But it remained largely unsettled, and "Iowa County" passed from territory to territory as new states were formed around it.

The only real settlements in Iowa were army forts, and it had no organized government when it was part of the Louisiana Territory or when it was included in Missouri Territory. In 1834 it was attached to Michigan and two years later to Wisconsin. Finally, in 1838, Iowa was made a separate territory.

A rush of settlers poured into the Iowa plains after the Black Hawk War lessened the threat of Indian attacks. Demands for statehood were voiced almost as soon as Iowa became a territory. A constitution was adopted in 1844, but Congress refused to accept the state boundaries that the Iowans had set. They, in turn, wouldn't accept the boundaries that Congress proposed. A compromise was reached at last and Iowa became a state in December 1846.

GEORGE JONES

(*1804–1896*)

George Wallace Jones perhaps more than any other man was responsible for making the laws that narrowed the vast Midwest plains into workable, state-size units.

He served Michigan when Iowa belonged to it, then Wisconsin when Iowa was part of that, and finally served Iowa itself when it became the rough rectangle of a state where he made his home.

Jones was born in Vincennes, Indiana, in 1804, but grew up in Missouri Territory, where his parents moved when he was a child. He went to school in St. Louis and then to college in Kentucky. One of his classmates at Transylvania University was Jefferson Davis, who later became President of the Confederate States. Another noted Southerner who befriended Jones while he was at college studying to become a lawyer was the already famous Senator Henry Clay.

When he graduated in 1825, Jones worked so hard at his lawbooks that his health broke under the strain. Doctors told him he should take to the outdoors to try to regain his strength. Adventuring north in his travels, he became a miner in Michigan Territory and then a village storekeeper. He met and married Josephine Gregoire and settled down at Sinsinawa.

It wasn't long, however, before Jones was seeking adventure again. He went soldiering against the Indians in the Black Hawk War and served as an aide to the courageous frontier military leader Henry Dodge. Through Dodge, he became familiar with the northwestern regions of Michigan Territory.

Jones entered politics and was sent to Congress as Michigans' territorial representative. During his first term in Washington, he succeeded in getting Congress to establish the northwestern lands as Wisconsin Territory. He returned to Congress for his second term as territorial representative from

Wisconsin instead of Michigan. Once again, he offered legislation to reduce the great land areas to a size that could be more easily governed. Jones was responsible for the creation of Iowa Territory in 1836.

In two years he had launched two areas toward the beginnings of eventual statehood. Still living in Wisconsin in 1838, he was a candidate for re-election from there. In his manners and habits, Jones was more a Southern gentleman than a north woods pioneer. True to those traditions, he acted as a second in a duel for a friend who felt his honor had been challenged. The publicity given the duel cost Jones the Wisconsin election.

He quit politics for a time and turned again to the outdoor life he had come to love. But when he was appointed surveyor general of the Wisconsin and Iowa territories, he soon found his two interests combined. As a man who had served so prominently in Congress, he could not ignore politics completely. He turned his attention more and more to Iowa, particularly during the years when Iowa's admission as a state depended on setting the very boundaries he was surveying.

Jones moved his family to Iowa and settled in Dubuque. There he was looked to for political leadership as well as for expert advice on the boundary questions. Active with him was Augustus Dodge, son of his old friend and army companion from Wisconsin, Henry Dodge. Together, Jones and the younger Dodge worked through the final year of constitutional revisions that were necessary to win Congressional approval for Iowa statehood.

When Iowa became a state in 1846, Jones and Dodge were elected its first two Senators. Jones represented Iowa in the United States Senate for twelve years. They were years of rapid growth when the railroads were pushing west and Jones, as sponsor of land grant bills that encouraged them, was responsible for bringing many of the lines into Iowa.

But Jones, always a Southerner in his outlook, became less popular at home as new settlers moved into Iowa and antislavery feelings grew. He failed to win re-election to the Senate in 1858. President Buchanan appointed him Minister to Colombia and he served brilliantly in the South American diplomatic post, where his charm won new friends for the United States.

When he returned to America in 1861 at the start of the Civil War years, Jones was arrested and charged with carrying on a treasonous correspondence with Jefferson Davis and other Confederate leaders. He was able to prove that the letters he wrote his old college classmate and Southern friends were no more dangerous to the Union than the usual friendly notes he had always exchanged with them. Jones was released on the direct orders of Abraham Lincoln.

He came back to Iowa to live, his adventuring over at last. Throughout the war he argued for tolerance, but Iowa was firmly a Union state and his opinions were ignored. Jones's political career was finished. Gradually, however, he was able to renew his personal friendships with those who had been close to him since Iowa's pioneer days.

His last years were lived happily as the bitterness of the Civil War eased with the passing of time. Once again, he received public respect from the state he had marked out. The legislature granted him a pension. On his ninetieth birthday he was given a reception by Iowa's General Assembly. Two years later, he died at his home in Dubuque, a state maker whose life had nearly spanned the nineteenth century.

TEXAS

Motto: Friendship

Flower: Bluebonnet

Bird: Mockingbird

Tree: Pecan

Admitted to the Union: 1845

☆

The Spanish and the French established colonies in early Texas, but the Indians kept settlers out of most of the area. Although long a part of the Spanish colony of Mexico, and then a province named for the Tejas Indians, the region wasn't really opened to permanent settlement until after Mexico's war for independence from Spain.

Stephen Austin, who grew up in Missouri, led American colonists into Texas in 1821. Other settlers followed and they established a provisional government in 1835 to throw off Mexican rule.

In March 1836, the historic defense of the Alamo, in which a small band of Texans battled to the death against an army of several thousand Mexicans, aroused all of Texas to fighting anger. Independence from Mexico already had been declared. A formal constitution was adopted eleven days after the fall of the Alamo. Six weeks later, the Mexicans were defeated at San Jacinto and the Republic of Texas was free. It remained a separate nation for nearly ten years.

Sam Houston, leader of the Texas army, was elected the first president and the republic quickly was recognized by the United States, Great Britain, France and Belgium. Plagued by Indian troubles and financial problems, many Texans sought union with the United States. But the act was delayed by Congressional arguments over the question of slavery until after President Polk was elected in 1844.

The following year, Congress invited Texas to become a state and Texas accepted. Mexico had never recognized Texas independence and regarded the American decision as a declaration of war by the United States. When the Mexican War ended, the treaty gave Texas land that later became part of five other states. In 1850 all this territory outside the present borders of Texas was turned over to the United States for ten million dollars.

SAMUEL HOUSTON
(1793–1863)

Samuel Houston might have stepped right out of the legends of the West to the pages of Texas history.

He was a giant of a man, both in figure and in the things he did. Dramatic in his actions and his personal moods, he was an adventurer whose own life often was in conflict between the ways of civilization and those of the Indians who adopted him and called him "brother."

Rockbridge County, near Lexington, Virginia, was the place of his birth, on March 2, 1793. His father was a Revolutionary War soldier who died when Sam was thirteen. He grew up in western Tennessee, where his mother took the family after his father's death. Compared with aristocratic Virginia, the settlement where they made their new home seemed the very outpost of civilization.

Young Sam loved the wilderness life. When his older brothers found him a job as a grocery clerk, he decided to run away from home. For several years he lived with the Cherokee Indians. Still in his teens, but by then more a man than a boy, he started a school for young children and improved his own education by going to an academy at Maryville.

The excitement of the War of 1812 took him from his books

to serve under Andrew Jackson in the battles against the Creek Indians. After the war, when the Cherokees in Tennessee were being resettled west of the Mississippi, he was appointed to help manage their removal.

But his sympathy for the Indians and the fact that he considered himself one of them brought official disapproval of some of his actions, especially when he appeared before the Secretary of War dressed in Indian clothes. He was sharply criticized and promptly resigned.

However, he had captured public attention. His outspoken manner, strong personality and flair for the dramatic led him into politics, and a bright future was predicted for him. He studied law, opened a law office in Lebanon, and rapidly moved up through various state positions to run for Congress.

Elected a Representative from Tennessee, he served in Washington for four years. In 1827 the people of Tennessee chose him for governor. Already his fame had spread beyond his own state. He was one of the promising young leaders of the Jackson Democrats and there was talk that Sam Houston was destined for a high place in the national government as a favorite son of Tennessee.

Happily Houston married Eliza Allen, and looked forward to almost certain re-election as governor. But three months after the wedding, his bride left him. In his heartbreak over the failure of his marriage, he resigned as governor. He quit Tennessee and everything in it to rejoin his Cherokees in Oklahoma.

The Indians granted him the retreat he sought from the hurts and disappointments of society. He lived among them as one of them, and they made him a full member of the tribe. Houston acted as their trader. But, as much as he wished to forget the world outside, he soon was on his way to Washington again.

He went, not as an elected representative, but as a spokesman for the Cherokees. Aroused by the frauds practiced against the Indians by government agents, Houston left his self-chosen retreat to expose them and to plead for an end to the injustices.

Because of Houston's unusual knowledge of Indian affairs, President Jackson commissioned him in 1832 to try to arrange treaties to protect American traders along the Mexican-Texas border. Still avoiding politics, he at first took no direct part in the growing demand for Texas independence from Mexico. But on one of his visits to Texas, he agreed to let his name be put on a ballot for delegates to a Texas convention and was unanimously elected.

The convention, held on April 1, 1833, appealed to Mexico to declare Texas a separate province and offered a constitution for Mexican approval. Santa Ana, the dictator of Mexico, refused and issued decrees to tighten his control. His dictatorial orders aroused Texans to plot complete independence.

By then, Sam Houston had cast his lot with the Texas settlers. Named a major general of the militia, he soon succeeded Stephen Austin as commander in chief.

The War for Texas Independence started with a series of skirmishes in which the ill-equipped and poorly trained Texans were heavily outnumbered by opposing Mexicans. Houston was criticized by the Texans themselves for the early defeats they suffered and had trouble holding together any kind of army at all.

After the bitter defeat at the Alamo, his forces numbered less than eight hundred men. They were raw troops, with little knowledge of organized warfare. About all they had was their courage and the fierce determination to make Texas free, a fighting spirit aroused by the cry "Remember the Alamo!"

They fell into retreat before Santa Ana's advancing army of twice as many well-trained veterans. Yet it was not a disorderly rout. Sam Houston planned the retreat with military cunning that led the Mexicans to where he could take them completely by surprise.

Santa Ana was overconfident of victory. The last thing he expected was a fresh attack. On the bank of the San Jacinto River, Houston turned his Texans to attack. They overcame the Mexicans, defeated them, and captured Santa Ana himself.

Houston, the hero of Texas, was elected the first president of the new independent republic. The constitution prevented him from holding the office for two successive terms, but he was elected president for a second time in 1841.

The new nation was harassed by border troubles and money problems. Many of the American settlers had looked toward linking Texas with the United States from the beginning of its struggle to break away from Mexico. Houston became a leader of the forces seeking annexation.

Patiently he guided his republic through the long period of diplomatic negotiations and of waiting while the slavery issue was debated in Washington. His second term as president of Texas expired just before James Polk was elected President of the United States on a platform that favored inviting Texas to become part of the Union.

In the election that followed formal admission of Texas as a state in 1845, Houston was chosen one of its first Senators. He served in Washington for fourteen years.

During the period just before the Civil War, he stood against the move for secession in Texas and was defeated for the Senate. Houston returned home, rallied the support of the voters on the basis of his own personal popularity, and was elected governor of Texas.

But the state was committed to the Southern cause and the legislature voted to join the states that left the Union. When Houston refused to swear allegiance to the Confederacy, he was removed from office as governor.

Northern friends offered him haven and assistance, but Houston refused their help. Even if his views were opposed to those of most of the people in Texas, he was a Texan and he wouldn't quit the land that he had helped to become a nation and then a state. Against the decision his people had made, he still abided by it.

He had stood up to trouble and criticism all his life. Old man that he was, he wouldn't run from it then, or seek the aid of others against the will of Texas. He retired to his home in Huntsville, where he died in 1863 at the age of seventy.

WISCONSIN

Motto: Forward

Flower: Violet   Bird: Robin

Tree: Sugar Maple

Admitted to the Union: 1848

☆

Early explorers visited Wisconsin in their search for the legendary Northwest Passage, which they hoped would be a way ships could sail across the inland waters of America to reach China. Then for nearly two hundred years after the first explorers came, the vast lands of Wisconsin remained mostly the home of the Indians.

There was a lively fur trade and some small settlements around scattered military outposts, but it wasn't until after treaties were made with the Indians in the early 1800's that the area really was opened to settlers. Then, almost at once, the population boomed.

Some came to seek the wealth of the lead mines that had been jealously guarded by the Indians. Many more flooded into Wisconsin to buy government land in the hope of selling it again for quick profit. The land speculators were followed by the true settlers who came into the wilderness and developed it. Within a dozen years, Wisconsin's population rose from almost nothing to more than a quarter of a million.

The settlers came from New England, New York, and the South, as well as from Europe into the melting pot of the new frontier—Yankees in prairie schooners, Germans with a few possessions from the fatherland, Irish, Dutch, Protestants and Catholics, radicals and conservatives. The trip from Boston to the lead mines cost only fifty dollars. A family of four could cross the Atlantic for a hundred dollars and reach Wisconsin for a hundred more. The same amount would buy an eighty-acre farm.

With them, they brought a dream of freedom and opportunity that leveled differences among them to build a state. Wisconsin had been part of Indiana, Illinois and Michigan territories before it became a separate territory in 1836. Within ten years, while the melting pot grew, an enabling act was passed. Two years later, in 1848, Wisconsin was admitted as the thirtieth of the United States.

HENRY DODGE
(1782–1867)

Henry Dodge was a true son of the frontier. Born in an Indian trader's cabin in Vincennes, Indiana, he spent his youth in pioneer Kentucky and grew to manhood in Missouri in the days when it was part of the real Wild West.

He sailed flatboats down the Mississippi, was a miner, cattleman, sheriff, soldier and peacemaker with the Indians before he became the governor who led Wisconsin from territory to statehood.

When he was only fourteen, according to stories later told about him, he had his first hand-to-hand combat with an Indian. His two-fisted adventuring sometimes led him into rough-and-tumble brawls that taught him personal courage. He always regretted his lack of formal schooling and became a life-long fighter for the right of every boy to a good free education, which had been denied to him.

His father, a Connecticut soldier of the Revolution, had moved west from New England to seek his fortune and to marry Nancy Ann Hunter, a heroine of Indian raids on the Kentucky frontier. The Dodge family struck out for the settlements beyond the Mississippi and Henry's father established himself at Ste. Genevieve, Missouri. He prospered there as a merchant, saltmaker and lead miner, and Henry went to work helping his father as soon as he was old enough to take a hand in the family enterprises.

Growing up on the frontier, he learned to make friends with men of all sorts, good and bad, settlers and Indians, people of many conflicting backgrounds. He made himself well liked among them and developed a talent for bringing together those whose ideas and ways of life often were far apart.

In 1800, while still working with his father at Ste. Genevieve, he married Christina McDonald, and became a deputy and then the sheriff of the district. As a Western lawman, he had to enforce order over men who sometimes tried to take the law into their own hands.

Serving as sheriff, Henry Dodge also commanded volunteer troops in putting down troubles with the Indians. In 1814, toward the close of the war with England, he led a detachment of several hundred soldiers to rescue the settlers at Boone's Lick. He later made several treaties with the Indians. His introduction to politics came in 1820 when he was sent as a delegate to the convention that framed the Missouri constitution.

Reports of mineral wealth in the lead mines of southwestern Wisconsin spread through the area. Dodge hadn't been doing so well with his own Missouri mining. He decided in 1827 to pull up stakes and take his family to the new fields. With his wife, nine children and four slaves, he moved to the settlement later named after him, Dodgeville, built a home and opened mines.

Soon he was mining as much as two thousand pounds of lead in a single day. He built the territory's first lead smelter and shipped his lead by river to New Orleans. Wisconsin was then a part of Michigan Territory and his holdings were a long way from the capital. He began to argue that the miners deserved a better voice in their faraway government.

The miners chose him to represent them in the territorial legislature at Detroit, but new Indian troubles kept him from attending the sessions. The Black Hawk War had begun and the whole lead-mining region was near panic. Dodge promptly took command of a force of troops to prevent the uprising from spreading. He helped to win one of the decisive battles of the war and restore the settlers' faith in the army to defend them.

As the panic ended, his fame as an Indian fighter grew. Dodge became a military hero, praised by the government in Washington, his courage celebrated in songs sung by his troops. The War Department organized a body of Mounted Rangers to patrol the whole frontier of growing settlements and President Jackson appointed Dodge to command them.

Within a year, he was commissioned a colonel and made leader of the United States Dragoons which became the famous Mounted Rifle Regiment. His Dragoons ranged the entire West, patrolling the settlements, traveling south in 1834 to visit Pawnee villages around the Arkansas and Red rivers, and the following summer scouting the Rocky Mountain region as far west as Colorado.

Dodge returned to his Wisconsin mines in the spring of 1836, just as the bill was signed to create a separate territory. President Jackson appointed him territorial governor and he took the oath of office on the Fourth of July. As age was reckoned on the frontier, he was already an old man of fifty-four when he began his new career in politics. But he went on to serve Wisconsin as a territory and a state for another twenty-one years.

From his first day in office, Dodge constantly championed the cause of statehood. He also fought against the land speculators. Many of the speculators laid out maps on which little crossroad villages were shown as great dream cities of the future. The villages battled among themselves over which of them should be chosen Wisconsin's capital.

In his first message to the first joint session of the legislature, Governor Dodge asked that some of the public land be sold to establish "an academy for the education of youth." His political enemies manipulated things so that Madison was chosen the capital, although the city didn't exist except on paper. Dodge then urged a tax on the landholdings of non-residents to pay for public schools.

Because of a shift in national politics, he was removed as governor of the territory in 1840 after he had declared that the speculators had a "withering influence on the best interests" of the community. But the people immediately chose him their territorial delegate to Congress, where he had a chance to work directly for statehood.

Four years later, he was reappointed territorial governor by President Polk, who praised him as "a pioneer of the West, an old Indian fighter, a man of high character and one of the common people." Once again, Dodge made it his first business to call for a revision of the school laws. Despite his own lack of formal schooling, he considered good public education the basis of true democracy.

He pressed for Wisconsin's admission as a state, but to bring it into the Union was no easy task. Many of the people were against taking on the cost and responsibility of state government. There were disputes over what would become Wisconsin's boundary lines and a fear of high taxes. More than a third of Wisconsin's settlers were foreign-born, with great differences of background and political opinion.

After Congress passed the enabling act, two stormy conventions were held to adopt a constitution. Delegates to the first convention debated for eleven weeks and produced a document so radical and liberal for its times that the voters flatly turned it down. The second constitutional convention was more conservative and the voters finally approved. The vote came in March and Congress formally admitted Wisconsin on May 29, 1848.

The people honored their longtime protector and leader, Henry Dodge, by electing him one of Wisconsin's first Senators. His son, Augustus Caesar Dodge, was serving as a Senator from Iowa at the same time. During their terms in the Senate together, father and son sometimes voted against each other. Henry Dodge was never known to let his personal feelings about any bill influence his vote.

He said he felt it was his duty to vote as the people of Wisconsin would want him to. Although he was a close associate of Webster, Clay, Douglas and other great orators of the Senate, Dodge was not an outstanding public speaker. But he was an able executive and a man who always held his own state first in his thoughts.

When his party's convention nominated him for the Vice-Presidency of the United States, he declined the honor. In 1857 he retired from the Senate at the age of seventy-five. President Pierce offered to name him Governor of Washington Territory, but because of his age, he also turned down that honor. His last years were spent quietly and happily with his son, Augustus, at Burlington, Iowa, where he lived to the age of eighty-five.

PART IV. BATTLES AND BOUNDARIES

CALIFORNIA

Motto: Eureka (I Have Found It)

Flower: Golden Poppy   Bird: Valley Quail

Tree: Redwood

Admitted to the Union: 1850

California was a Mexican territory when the first real push of American settlement began. The overland trails brought Easterners to the Far West in growing numbers in the 1840's and some of them worked with the Spanish Californians to overthrow Mexican rule.

Pathfinder John Frémont and the Americans set up a republic under the Bear Flag, which lasted a short time before word reached California of the war between the United States and Mexico. In July 1846, Commodore John Sloat captured the capital at Monterey and claimed California for the United States. The next year, General Stephen Kearny claimed a land victory and in 1848 the treaty with Mexico formally made California an American possession.

That was the year James Marshall made his discovery of gold and started men from all over the world rushing toward California to try their luck at finding it. The '49ers came in droves to the roaring mine camps that often boomed into cities almost overnight. There wasn't much in the way of government or law, except for military control.

Because of the national balance between free and slave states, Congress delayed making California a territory. General Bennet Riley, who was in command of the occupying troops, decided something had to be done to give the people orderly self-government. As a result of his decisive action, California declared itself a state ten months before it was admitted to the Union.

BENNET RILEY
(1787–1851)

General Bennet Riley was an old man of sixty-one when he arrived at Monterey to take charge of the American occupation. His army career had begun more than thirty-five years before, a whole continent away in New York, during the battles of the War of 1812. He was a tired man, a weary warrior, and glad there was peace to be found in California.

The people of the little red and white Spanish village, who had seen four different flags fly above them, welcomed the American soldiers and the general who would be their temporary governor. He himself hoped he wouldn't be in charge of the government for very long.

Not much is known about Bennet Riley's boyhood or his years of growing up. Born in St. Mary's County, Maryland, in 1787, he was twenty-six years old before he enlisted in an army rifle company. After action in New York, his company was sent to the Mississippi frontier, where he served against the British and Indians and rose to the rank of captain. He transferred to the infantry and, for the next quarter century, faced the hardships and dangers of frontier military life.

Riley fought Indians in the Dakotas, commanded troops that convoyed merchant caravans across the Santa Fe Trail, showed his bravery in the Black Hawk War and then in the war against the Seminoles in Florida. Promoted through the ranks to major general, he led his brigade in the war with Mexico and took over posts in Louisiana and Missouri before being put in charge of American forces in California.

He was a man who had spent his long life in action and was impatient of delay. Many people had hoped California would be made a territory almost as soon as it was taken from Mexico. But month after month went by while Congress debated the issue in Washington and made no decision as to how the area was to be governed.

With so many settlers pouring in, lawlessness and disorder threatened to grow. The old Spanish and Mexican laws were little use and military control was a poor substitute for orderly self-government. In some of the brawling mine camps and booming new towns, citizens organized their own committees to try to enforce whatever makeshift regulations they chose to call the law.

Bennet Riley decided he had to be the one to act, if Congress would not, to put American government into effect. On June 3, 1849, he issued a proclamation calling on the people to declare for themselves whether they wanted to make California a territory or a state. He asked for delegates to be chosen, either to plan for a territorial government or to form a state constitution.

That September, forty-eight elected delegates met at Monterey in a hall that had been built only a short time before. Skipping the usual step of first becoming a territory, the Californians went to work to build themselves a state. A little more than one month later, they finished writing a constitution. It was ratified in November and state officers were elected the same day.

Still acting with a speed dictated by the increasing numbers of gold seekers flooding into the area, the legislature convened on December 15th and within one week chose state officials, supreme court justices, and elected California's first Senators. Peter H. Burnett was inaugurated Governor.

There was no provision in either the military or civil law that gave General Riley the right to set up a state government for California. His calm decision, more far-reaching than any the old warrior had ever made in the heat of battle, was followed by a briefly worded announcement to the effect that the new state simply did exist.

In that final proclamation as military governor, issued on December 20, 1849, Riley declared: "A new executive having been elected and installed into office in accordance with the provisions of the Constitution of the State, the undersigned hereby resigns his powers as Governor of California."

He was the highest-ranking United States official on the scene and his recognition of California's government was enough to put that government into operation. There was still much debate and angry argument when the news reached Washington that California had invited itself into the Union as a free state. But Congress finally approved the admission on September 9, 1850.

Riley was ordered to new army duty near the Rio Grande River. It was an assignment he was unable to fulfill. His action in California had been his last. Doctors discovered his tiredness was more than he himself had realized. He had helped a new state find birth, but he was already a dying man, stricken with an illness which left him only two more years to live.

Although they were physically painful years, they also were years of happiness for Bennet Riley. After most of his lifetime spent helping to open up the West, he lived for that one short period as an ordinary husband and father with his wife and children, before death finally came to him at his home in Buffalo, New York.

MINNESOTA

Motto: The North Star

Flower: Moccasin Flower   Bird: Loon

Tree: Norway Pine

Admitted to the Union: 1858

☆

Minnesota's glacier-made land of thousands of lakes and towering timber, spaced by stretching prairies, was the home of warring tribes of Indians and a center of the great Northwest fur trade until the army opened the way for settlers to move in.

The establishment of Fort Snelling, started in 1819 as a military outpost on the frontier, extended American authority over the region and began to change the wilderness into the farms and towns that would become a state.

Lumber camps began to dot the pine forests and the settlements grew. In 1848 the first big land boom came, and enough people had moved into Minnesota within a year to organize territorial government. Roads were built, large tracts of public land were surveyed and sold, and St. Paul, at the head of navigation on the Mississippi, became the commercial center where steamboats unloaded goods and settlers. Other river towns flourished as prosperous ports of entry.

Steamboats sometimes brought in whole colonies to settle an entire townsite at once. The territorial government set up an immigration board to attract people, and transportation agencies encouraged new settlements. Within six years, there were twenty-five times as many people in Minnesota as there had been when it became a territory.

In 1857 Congress passed a bill to enable Minnesota to

become a state. It was a time of bitter political rivalry between Democrats and Republicans. When the elected delegates gathered in St. Paul to draft Minnesota's constitution, the Democrats and Republicans refused to sit together in the same room.

As a result, each party held separate sessions in different rooms of the first capitol building. The two bodies never acted together during the entire convention. Five members from each party exchanged ideas and reported to their respective groups and a compromise finally was worked out.

Two almost identical constitutions were drawn up. The Democrats would not sign the Republican one and the Republicans refused to have their names on a constitution that bore the signatures of Democrats. The solution gave Minnesota two separate constitutions, one written on white paper and signed only by Republicans and the other on blue-tinted paper signed only by Democrats.

Both copies were sent to Washington. The Democratic version was attached to the bill to admit Minnesota to the Union, but historians report that when the measure came back from the Senate, the Republican version somehow had been substituted. Meanwhile, the people of Minnesota unanimously accepted the constitution in the next election and went ahead to choose their state officers. The legislature passed two amendments that were ratified by the voters and Congress approved in May 1858.

Today, Minnesota is unique among the states in that it has two constitutions instead of one, both almost identical and both preserved by the Archives Commission as evidence of the state's fundamental law.

HENRY SIBLEY

(1811–1891)

Henry Sibley came to Minnesota when it was a wilderness and helped to make it a territory and then a state. Pioneer settler, hunter, trapper and fur trader, he also was a man with a vision of the future who was able to lead other men through a half century of political growth to realize the dream of self-government.

Born in Detroit, in Michigan Territory, in 1811, he was far from being a typical backwoodsman. His father was a Michigan delegate to Congress and later a territorial supreme court judge. On his mother's side, he was related to Abraham Whipple, renowned naval hero of the Revolution.

Sibley had a remarkably good education for a frontier boy. He went to an academy at Detroit and then was given private schooling in the classics and two years' study of law, which he finished by the time he was seventeen. But for all his book learning, he was an adventurous youth and he quit Detroit in the summer of 1828 to take a job at Fort Brady in far northern Michigan.

Working behind the counter in the sutler's store, he sold food and supplies to soldiers and Indian traders. The next spring, he became a clerk for the American Fur Company at Mackinac, which then dominated the Northwestern fur trade. Company agents traveled through the whole wilderness area, arranging deals with trappers and Indians, and Sibley not only learned the business, but also gained an exciting first-hand knowledge of the lore of the north woods.

Promoted to the office at Cleveland, Ohio, he was put in charge of purchasing the company's entire supply of necessities, ranging from flour, corn, pork and dried meats to tobacco and other staples. Two veteran fur trappers asked him to become their partner in operating one of the company's outposts that had exclusive rights to trade with the Sioux Indians all the way to the Canadian border and west to the Rocky Mountains.

He accepted at once and started the journey in the summer of 1834, as soon as he could get together the supplies he would need. Traveling sometimes on horseback, but mostly on foot and by canoe, he arrived four weary months later at Mendota, a place in Minnesota which was under the protection of Fort Snelling. It wasn't a village then, or even a real settlement, but just a grouping of primitive shelters for trappers and traders.

It was there that Henry Sibley built himself a house of imposing size, "a substantial and commodious stone dwelling," which was the first private residence in all of Minnesota and Dakota. From the time it was completed, the doors were opened wide in warm hospitality to every person who visited Minnesota. His visitors included explorers, travelers, missionaries, Indians, trappers, traders—and later the first incoming settlers.

Sibley made friends among them all and as his fame grew as a genial host, so did his influence. He won the respect of the Sioux Indians as well. As the fur company's representative, he had the power to decide how much the Indians would earn for their furs. He treated them fairly and won their respect for him as a person as well as for his skill as a hunter and a woodsman.

He was still a young man of twenty-two when he married Sarah Jane Steele and brought her to his big stone house to live. Mendota and other Minnesota settlements had begun to grow by then and the formation of other states had created a political no man's land. When Wisconsin and then Iowa set their boundaries, the whole area from the St. Croix River west to the Missouri and White Earth rivers was left without territorial government of its own.

Sibley and other settlers held a convention in August 1849 to seek a separate territory, which they asked to have named Minnesota. That October, he was elected to Congress as a delegate. He was admitted to his Congressional seat in January and immediately went to work with Illinois' Senator Stephen Douglas, chairman of the Committee on Territories, to secure passage of the act. Two months later, Sibley succeeded and the territory was established.

The population of the new territory was about six thousand, but what had been a slow growth of settlement suddenly became a boom. Commercial steamboating began on the Minnesota River. Treaties with the Indians opened the region west of the Mississippi to settlers. Immigration societies were formed and farm organizations encouraged the bringing in of blooded stock and choice seeds, grains and fruit trees for farms. Railroads moved closer to the Mississippi and real estate operators moved far ahead of them to create a clamoring demand for towns.

When Henry W. Longfellow's poem "Song of Hiawatha," inspired by Minnesota Indian legends, was published in 1855, it encouraged many hundreds more to seek homes in the beautiful land of the "sky blue waters." All the publicity and promotion by many agencies of government and transportation multiplied the Minnesota-bound settlers until the soaring population passed 150,000.

Sibley and other territorial leaders realized the advantages that statehood might bring. For one thing, there would be the land grants that Congress could be expected to make only to states. Another urgent matter was the growth of the railroads that soon would bring a need for a stronger voice in Washington to urge the building of a route to the Pacific through Minnesota.

Minnesota again found a friend in Senator Stephen Douglas and, with his support, the enabling act passed Congress in 1857. Sibley presided over the Democratic delegates to the divided constitutional convention. His influence between sessions did much to help bring the rival political groups into compromise so that the committees of Democrats and Republicans could frame a document both sides would accept.

He was elected the new state's first governor, but the political battle was so close he edged out his Republican opponent by less than three hundred votes. In the next election he decided not to be a candidate. However, Minnesota soon had need of his leadership again, not as a politician but as a frontiersman.

With the outbreak of the Civil War, the Sioux Indians, who had been peaceful for years, goaded by a lack of food and neglect of government payments due to them, saw a chance to rise up against the settlers. Army forts were beseiged and homes and settlements attacked. More than five hundred people were massacred.

Sibley, acting as general of the state troops, marched from St. Paul with an ill-equipped band of soldiers and almost no cavalry support. His forces brought relief to the frontier outposts, engaged the Indians in several furious battles, and finally won a decisive victory at Wood Lake. Sibley arranged for the release of captives and then headed an expedition that drove the remaining Sioux warriors beyond the Missouri. He was appointed a commissioner to negotiate the treaties of peace.

With the state he had helped to create, build and protect, calm once again, and with the frontier that he had known as a young man changed into the peaceful towns that were growing to cities, Sibley was ready to retire. But retirement for him meant a still-active life.

He became president of a St. Paul gas company, of an insurance company, and director of a bank. For many years, he served as head of the Board of Regents of the University of Minnesota. And in 1871, when he was sixty, he once again had a brief fling at politics and sat for one term in the state legislature. He lived to the age of eighty, a powerful and influential figure in Minnesota.

OREGON

Motto: The Union

Flower: Oregon Grape

Bird: Western Meadow Lark

Tree: Douglas Fir

Admitted to the Union: 1859

☆

Oregon settlers established the first American government on the Pacific Coast. It had no connection with the government in Washington and was on land that didn't even belong to the United States. Eleven years later, Oregon did become a territory and in six more years, a state. But the provisional government of 1842 was a stepping stone that made the jump from wilderness to civilization a little easier.

When the War of 1812 began, American fur traders who had a small settlement at Astoria sold out to the British fur traders in the area because they knew there would be no way to defend their holdings. The treaty that ended the war gave Britain and the United States equal rights to the region, but British interests remained stronger.

Gradually settlers started to come from America to Oregon not for furs, but to build farms and homes. Although there was no real government, none seemed needed, for the settlers lived peaceably enough. Their numbers began to grow in the early 1840's, however, and they wanted clear title to the lands where they hoped to remain and establish towns. This was impossible under the loose joint rule of two nations.

In 1842 the new pioneers called a meeting at Champoeg. The group was about equally divided between British and Americans. When their 102 votes were counted, 52 were in favor of having American rule. The Champoeg delegates, acting on their own authority, went ahead and established a firm provisional government.

Meanwhile both nations were anxious to end joint control and settle on a boundary line. The British wanted the line set at the Columbia River, but the Americans insisted on a boundary farther north. The slogan "Fifty-four Forty or Fight" became a campaign issue of the 1844 election.

By a treaty drawn in 1846, the northern boundary of the United States finally was set at the latitude of forty-nine degrees, the northern limit of what is now Washington State. But the settlers still had no government except the one they had created for themselves.

Oregon's most tragic Indian raid, the Whitman Massacre, took place the following year and the provisional government sent a spokesman to plead with Congress for Federal Government control and the protection of federal law and order.

The man they sent, one of Oregon's first permanent settlers, had helped to form the Champoeg convention and his own daughter had been one of the women tortured in the Whitman Massacre. His name was Joe Meek.

JOSEPH MEEK
(1810–1875)

Joseph L. Meek, uneducated fur trapper, farmer, practical joker and teller of tall tales, stormed across the continent from Oregon to the nation's capital. He arrived dirty, ragged and determined that Congress should hear him and act to establish a territorial government where it was needed.

And if Congress didn't act, Joe Meek said he would go down the road and see his "cousin-by-marriage, Jamie," and find out what he could do. "Jamie" was President James Polk and whether he was really Joe Meek's cousin or not didn't matter. The people of Washington loved Joe Meek. They called him "colonel" and gathered in crowds just to watch him and to listen to the fabulous tales he told.

Because of his tall tales, fact and fiction have become a little mixed up in his personal history. But even allowing for the way he liked to exaggerate things, his story remains a colorful and almost classic account of life on the frontier.

He was born in Virginia about 1810 and claimed in later years that his father had been a wealthy slaveholding plantation owner. As a child, he was stubborn, lazy and headstrong and admitted that he resisted both work and learning. He could neither read nor write at the age of sixteen. When he was eighteen he ran away from home.

Joe Meek arrived in St. Louis in the fall of 1828 and worked through the winter to get a stake. The next spring, he set out with an expedition bound for the mountains. For the next eleven years after he left civilization behind him, he roamed the Western mountains and plains, trading, trapping, guiding, mining, and fighting Indians and loneliness.

But he stored up a lifetime of storytelling out of those eleven years spent with men who were making frontier history. His roaming adventures led him from the Canadian wilds to the torrid deserts of Mexico and from the Missouri to the Pacific.

By the time he decided he finally should settle down, in 1840, he was nearing middle age. He and a friend, Robert Newell, chose some land on a bank of the Willamette River in Oregon, near what is now Portland. Although he had lived by the self-made laws of the wilderness most of his life until then, he became a champion of the cause to bring orderly government to Oregon.

He helped other Americans to settle in the new land and was one of those who called for a joint convention of British and American settlers to meet down the Willamette River at Champoeg. Before the convention, the Americans held a separate meeting and so did the British. When the joint meeting began, the rivalry between the two groups threatened to throw the whole gathering into confusion.

Joe Meek demonstrated that he was as keen a politician as

he was a trail guide. Just when the meeting seemed about to break up in fights and hard feelings without getting anything done, he called for a vote to declare the sentiments of those present.

The count showed that fifty-two favored American government and fifty sided with the British. Realizing that they were in the minority, some of the British settlers got up and walked out of the meeting. Those who remained then were able to get down to the work of naming a committee to draft laws. Their recommendations were adopted at a second convention two months later.

Because the only pattern they could find was a copy of the laws of Iowa, the lawmakers of the new government based their regulations on that. The people accepted the provisional government, elected local officials, and named Joe Meek their sheriff. He also was twice elected to the legislature.

The Whitman Massacre of 1847 brought to a head Oregon's desire for recognition as a federal territory. Marcus Whitman, pioneer missionary who had started a school and hospital, was savagely struck down by Indians who came seeking medicine, and others in the Whitman settlement were tortured and killed. The tragedy shocked all of Oregon into calling for federal protection. But Joe Meek had a deeper personal reason for seeking action in his grief over a daughter who was one of the victims.

Chosen by the Oregonians to go to Washington and plead their cause, he started his journey on January 4, 1848. He called attention to Oregon's plight as neither territory nor possession to all he met along the way by proclaiming himself the "envoy of the Republic of Oregon to the Court of the United States." It was May before he arrived in the nation's capital, where his appearance quickly gained him public attention.

Joe Meek symbolized the frontiersman in his looks as well as in his manner, and it was a natural role that he played to the hilt. Well over six feet tall, muscular and sturdily built, he had a bearded face, twinkling dark eyes and a melodious voice that held his listeners entranced as he spun his tales. He spoke with a Western dialect that might have been partly put on because people expected it.

He used his deliberate clowning to put across the appeal he had come to make and he told Oregon's story with conviction. In the last hours of the last day of that session of Congress, legislation was passed to allow Oregon to establish territorial government. On the same day, Joe Meek's "down the road" cousin-by-marriage, President James Polk, named General Joseph Lane governor of the new territory and chose Meek himself as United States Marshal.

When he returned to Oregon as marshal, he brought to justice five Indian chiefs convicted of taking part in the Whitman Massacre. He also served for a brief time as a major of frontier troops that put down another Indian uprising.

But Joseph Meek spent most of the remainder of his life quietly farming his own land and enjoying the home he had found in Oregon before he had helped to make Oregon part of the United States.

KANSAS

Motto: To the Stars Through Difficulties

Flower: Sunflower   Bird: Western Meadow Lark

Tree: Cottonwood

Admitted to the Union: 1861

☆

In 1830 Kansas was made part of the Indian Territory, set aside to be the home of the Indians forever. But people pushed into it from the borders, and only twenty-four years later Kansas became a separate territory. Senator Stephen A. Douglas of Illinois gave Kansas its name when he introduced the Kansas-Nebraska Bill to repeal the Missouri Compromise and to let settlers of the area decide for themselves whether to allow slavery.

Kansas became a battleground between settlers who rushed in from the North and South to try to win control of it. The violence and political troubles within Kansas affected the whole United States. During the seven years from territory to statehood, when it was called "Bleeding Kansas," the Federal Government named ten different governors or acting governors.

It had separate groups of proslavery and free-state officials and legislatures. Four attempts were made to provide a state constitution and win admission to the Union, which finally came on the eve of the Civil War.

During the same troubled years, settlers also changed Kansas from wilderness to civilization. The first of them took farming lands and were soon followed by men organizing town companies. When Kansas was made a territory in 1854, it was an unorganized domain, without laws or officers of its own, a place where there were two army posts, a dozen missions and some straggling settlements, with a total population of about fifteen hundred people.

Seven years later, when it became a state, the population had passed the 100,000 mark. There were more than 150 towns and forty counties in existence. Roads and bridges had been laid out, schools and a banking system had been set up, commerce had been established, several hundred churches had been built, public lands had been surveyed and nearly two million acres of farmland were being worked by private owners. Eleven thousand residents of the new state could claim they had been born in Kansas.

CHARLES ROBINSON
(1818–1894)

Charles Robinson first saw the wild Indian country of Kansas as a pioneer on the long overland trail toward the gold fields of California. He and his companions camped one night at the place that later became the city of Lawrence. Taking a look around, so the story goes, he told his fellow '49ers that would be a good spot for a future town. He pointed to a nearby hill and remarked that someday a great academy of learning might be established there.

Robinson, born in Massachusetts, had been a doctor and the head of a hospital in Springfield. After his first wife died, he decided to give up his medical practice and take off with a party of Bostonians seeking adventure in the West. When they reached California, he set out at once for the diggings at Bear Creek.

But two weeks of pick-and-shovel mining cured him of gold fever. All he dug up was plain dirt and he decided his fortunes lay elsewhere. The other miners did have to eat and there was money to be made serving them, so the doctor who had become a disillusioned gold miner set up a restaurant in Sacramento.

Robinson was a popular man and one not afraid to fight for a political cause. Before long, he was chosen by other settlers to head their association in their quarrels with land speculators. He was shot during a riot against town officials and was so badly wounded it was feared he would die.

Arrested and put aboard a prison ship in the harbor, Robinson unexpectedly recovered. By then, he was something of a hero among the miners and settlers and they elected him to the California legislature. He was released on bail and the charges against him finally were dropped.

In the legislature, Robinson had a hand in making California a free state and in drafting laws to break up the large Spanish land grants into small farms. He also voiced his strong views against slavery and for a time became editor of a Sacramento newspaper.

But in 1851 he tired of California and returned to Massachusetts by way of Panama to take up medicine again, and to marry for the second time. Although he tried to settle down to being a doctor, he couldn't forget his visions of the West and of the towns that someday might grow across the unsettled plains.

His wife, Sara Lawrence, shared his ambitions and encouraged his interest in Kansas. He took to writing again and for two years was editor of the *Fitchburg News*. Kansas already had become a burning political issue. Missourians, most of whom favored slavery, had begun to push across the borders of the Indian Territory. Whether Kansas eventually became a free or slave state would depend on the will of those who settled there.

Eli Thayer, the principal of a Massachusetts school for girls, had set up an organization called the New England Emigrant Aid Company to encourage free-staters to go to Kansas. Money for it was raised among wealthy New Englanders. Robinson and his wife volunteered their services. He already had been through Kansas, knew the West as a California pioneer, and Thayer appointed him resident agent in Kansas for the Emigrant Aid Company.

The Company sent Robinson to Kansas in 1854, just after it became a separate territory. He explored the fertile valleys, chose land that would make good farms, and selected sites for future towns. Then he went to St. Louis to meet the first group of emigrants from New England and also conducted a second party of free-state settlers into the territory. They founded the town of Lawrence and Robinson built a house on the hill he had pointed out on his way to seek gold in California. It was the place where the University of Kansas grew in later years.

That spring of 1855, Robinson was busy organizing the free-staters to take part in the election of a territorial legislature. Missourians and others from the South were increasing in numbers and already had founded the proslavery towns of Atchison and Leavenworth. There were no laws to decide who could vote and the polls were open to just about anybody who happened to be in Kansas to cast a ballot, no matter how short a time he had been there.

On election day a horde of Missourians crossed the border to vote. Some of them used pistols and knives to drive out election judges. There were also illegal free-state voters, but far more Missourians, and the proslavery forces won a big majority. A census count showed there were about three thousand men old enough to vote in the whole area, but more than twice that number of votes were cast.

Robinson and the free-staters refused to accept the authority of the new legislature or to obey its laws. They called it a "bogus legislature" and set up a provisional state government of their own. It drew up a state constitution, elected a separate legislature and state officers, and chose Robinson as governor. But while the free state legislature met and enacted laws, it had no way to enforce them and no money to support itself.

The proslavery legislature was recognized as the legal one by the Federal Government, Congress voted money for it, and it had soldiers at its command if it needed them. Robinson wrote to the New England Emigrant Aid Company and asked for weapons, and some of the members privately shipped rifles and small cannon to the free-staters. News that they were arming themselves angered the proslavery group.

Bitterness grew throughout the summer and autumn and finally exploded in violence. Men were killed, others were tarred and feathered, seized by mobs and warned to leave the territory. Robinson was indicted for treason and was captured in Missouri while he was on his way East to obtain more help. He was brought back and put into prison at Lecompton, where he was held for four months awaiting trial.

Homes were burned, there were shootings from ambush, and some settlers took to the woods and fields to hide or to strike down their enemies. The whole nation became aroused over "Bleeding Kansas," fearing open warfare if the violence wasn't stopped.

When the proslavery forces called up the state troops to advance on Lawrence and burn it to ashes, federal soldiers had to be summoned from Fort Leavenworth. They disbanded both the militia and the free-state men and President Pierce ordered the release of the treason prisoners held at Lecompton.

Meanwhile, the constitution adopted by the free-staters at Topeka had been put before Congress in a move to gain acceptance of Kansas as a state. The House of Representatives voted for it, but when it came into the Senate it was rejected because the proslavery group had not taken part in the writing of it.

The proslavery group also had written a constitution at Lecompton, but the free-staters had refused to vote on that. When it came before Congress the free-staters tried to prove that it had been forced through by fraud. The Senate voted for it, but the House referred it back to the people of Kansas.

Almost admitted first as a free state and then as a slave state, Kansas finally held another convention and drew up a constitution at Wyandotte in which all parties took part. By then, the free-staters outnumbered the proslavery settlers. They voted for the Wyandotte constitution, named Topeka the temporary capital, and elected Charles Robinson governor of the new state.

Kansas still had to wait more than a year before it was admitted by Congress. Lincoln, as the candidate of the Republican Party, urged the admission and when he was elected President most of the Southern states began to leave the Union. As each state withdrew, this reduced the number left in Congress to oppose Kansas.

Lincoln did not take office until March 1861. In January of that year, James Buchanan signed the bill that made Kansas a state. The news was telegraphed to the *Leavenworth Conservative,* a newspaper founded only the day before, and copies of the extra paper put out were stuffed into the saddlebags of riders who sped to Lawrence, where the legislature was in session. Cannons were fired in salute, and there was wild rejoicing as the news spread.

On his way to Washington in March to be inaugurated President, Abraham Lincoln stopped in Philadelphia and hoisted to the mast of Independence Hall the first flag to fly the thirty-fourth star. The trouble Kansas had in gaining statehood suggested the state's motto: "To the stars through difficulties."

There were still difficulties for the new state, mostly in raising money to operate it, and Robinson was threatened with impeachment over the financial troubles. Cleared of the charges, he finished out his one term as elected governor, later served as a state lawmaker, and became a leader of the efforts to bring good schools and education to the people of Kansas. He was seventy-six and his state was thirty-three years old when he died.

WEST VIRGINIA

Motto: Mountaineers Always Free

Flower: Rhododendron

Bird: Cardinal

Tree: Sugar Maple

Admitted to the Union: 1863

☆

West Virginia was the Civil War offspring of its parent state, Virginia. Long before the war, the small farmers and tradesmen of Virginia's western counties felt that state laws favored the large plantation owners of the Tidewater region. The Westerners claimed they were unfairly taxed and were not given an equal voice in Virginia's government.

Feelings between the two sections of Virginia became sharply divided over the slavery issue when abolitionist John Brown raided the arsenal at Harper's Ferry in western Virginia just before the Civil War. At the first Virginia convention to consider seceding from the Union, the western delegates helped defeat the motion. But a second convention met five days after South Carolina fired on Fort Sumter and voted to secede.

The western delegates against secession held a secret meeting before they left Richmond and vowed to "keep Virginia, or as much of her as possible, loyal to the Union," as well as to seek an eventual break with the parent state.

With a campaign cry of "New Virginia, now or never," the Westerners held two conventions at Wheeling. The first weighed the steps that would have to be taken to form a separate state and the second declared the parent state of Virginia no longer had a legal government because it had left the Union.

The delegates formed a "restored Virginia" and the people of the western counties voted to create a new state. The new constitution was ratified by President Lincoln, who issued a proclamation on April 20, 1863, that West Virginia would be admitted at the end of sixty days.

FRANCIS PIERPONT
(1814–1899)

Francis Harrison Pierpont "captured" the state of Virginia in the early days of the Civil War without firing a shot and carried it across the Blue Ridge Mountains. At the end of the war, he left a new state west of the mountains and "took" Virginia back to Richmond.

His father's family had settled just below the Pennsylvania border in western Virginia before the Revolution. Francis was born at the family homestead at Morgantown in 1814 but the Pierponts soon moved to Fairmont, where Francis grew up helping his father run their farm and tannery.

Francis was twenty-one before he felt he could be spared from the farm. He had no money for further education, but he was determined to get it. He set out with only the few belongings he could carry and walked 180 miles north to Meadville, Pennsylvania. There he worked his way through Allegheny College and graduated with honors in 1839. For the next few years, he taught school in Virginia frontier villages. When he was twenty-seven he went to Mississippi to teach for a year, but was called home because of his father's poor health.

The Pierponts, like other small farmers of the region, were burdened by what they felt were unjust taxes. Francis, seeking some way to improve things for his family and neighbors, read law in the time he could spare from teaching and was admitted to the bar. In 1848 he was appointed local attorney for the Baltimore and Ohio Railroad, then planning to bring its tracks into western Virginia. By the time the railroad reached Fairmont, he and a friend managed to get together the funds to open the area's first coal mine.

It was the beginning of boom times for a section that had long been poor and Francis Pierpont soon was a prosperous businessman. He married Julia Robertson of New York, brought her to his new home in the center of Fairmont, and was looked up to as a leading citizen who began to take a more active interest in politics. As the Civil War drew near he became an outspoken foe of slavery.

When Virginia voted to secede, Pierpont was among those who vowed to keep as much of the state as possible in the Union. He helped organize the two Wheeling conventions. At the end of the second one, he was elected governor of "restored Virginia."

He at once called for a session of the General Assembly to meet in Wheeling. The session was made up of members of the Virginia legislature from the western counties who were loyal to the Union. Because the parent Virginia government had withdrawn from the United States to join the Confederacy, Pierpont's government was recognized by President Lincoln and Congress as the only valid one.

This was a necessary step in creating West Virginia because the Constitution specified that "no new state shall be formed or erected within the jurisdiction of any other state . . . without the consent of the legislatures of the states concerned, as well as of the Congress."

As far as the North was concerned, the legal government of Virginia was the one represented by Pierpont and it gave its consent to separate statehood. Delegates met in Wheeling November 26, 1861, to form a constitution. It was promptly ratified by the western counties. For two more years, Pierpont headed the government of what still was considered "restored Virginia" from his office in Wheeling.

Nine days after President Lincoln's proclamation admitting West Virginia to the United States, Confederate troops reached Fairmont and threatened to burn Pierpont's house to the ground. He was in Wheeling at the time, but his neighbor, a widow who lived alone, persuaded them that if they started a fire her house also would be destroyed. The soldiers finally spared Pierpont's house, but made a large bonfire of the books in his law library as well as his papers and many personal belongings.

As soon as the elected officials of the new state of West Virginia assumed their duties, Pierpont left Wheeling for Alexandria. He set up the offices of "restored Virginia" in Alexandria until after the surrender of the Confederacy and then moved them to Richmond.

Pierpont tried hard to serve all the people of Virginia, whose government he had "captured," held through the war and finally returned. He was against many of the severe policies of other Northerners who wanted to punish the defeated South. His middle-of-the-road policy pleased nobody. Finally he was removed and replaced by a military governor in 1868.

He retired to Fairmont and served one term in the West Virginia state legislature and was appointed Collector of Internal Revenue under President Garfield. Nearly thirty years after giving up the governorship of the "restored" state of Virginia, Pierpont left West Virginia to live with a daughter in Pittsburgh, Pennsylvania, where he died on March 24, 1899.

NEVADA

Motto: All for Our Country

Flower: Sagebrush   Bird: Mountain Bluebird (unofficial)

Tree: Single-leaf Piñon

Admitted to the Union: 1864

☆

The early maps of North America showed Nevada as part of "the Great American Desert." It was a place people crossed on their way somewhere else. Trappers, miners, soldiers and then westward-bound wagon trains went across it. Finally, at about the time the region became part of the United States by treaty with Mexico, some Mormons settled down to stay.

The land was included in Utah Territory and settlers who considered themselves too far away from the seat of government made several attempts to form a government of their own. In 1854 the area was set apart as Carson County.

Five years later when the Comstock Lode was discovered and the news spread that the earth was filled with silver, the population boomed with a rush of prospectors. Utah Territory was divided and Nevada Territory was established in 1861.

Nevada tried to become a state in 1863. A convention of delegates framed a constitution, but the people voted it down because of the tax that was put on mines. The same voters who rejected the constitution did elect state officials, but left them with no offices to fill.

However, with the Civil War turning in favor of the North, national Republican Party leaders wanted to add two solid votes to their strength in the Senate, so they let it be known that a new application for statehood from Nevada would be looked upon with favor. President Lincoln signed an enabling act on March 21, 1864, and a revised version of the state constitution was accepted by Nevada's voters.

In an extravagant gesture to celebrate becoming a state, the full text of the constitution was sent over the new telegraph wires to President Lincoln in Washington. It was the longest telegram ever sent up to that time and cost nearly $3,500. The President gave his approval and issued a proclamation on October 31, 1864, declaring Nevada the thirty-sixth of the United States.

JAMES NYE
(1814–1876)

James Warren Nye was appointed territorial governor of Nevada, mostly as a political reward for his strong support of the Republican Party in New York State during the presidential election of 1860. But he turned out to be a man of action as well as one of silver-voiced charm. He gave the people of Nevada orderly self-government and made prompt decisions that led them to statehood.

Nye's lieutenant governor was a little-known lawyer from Iowa, Orion Clemens, whose brother came with him to the new territory, hoping for some minor political job. In Nevada, however, the brother went to work for a newspaper and chose another name for signing his stories: Mark Twain. Many of Twain's stories are based on Nevada's territorial days and early statehood under Governor Nye.

Nye was born in 1814 in Madison County, New York. His family had very little money and he had to work hard for his education. He studied law at Hamilton and practiced there. Without success he campaigned as a Democrat for a seat in Congress. He served as a county judge and then moved to Syracuse, where he became police commissioner in 1857.

With the approach of the Civil War, Nye's political views changed and he was an enthusiastic supporter of Lincoln as a candidate for President. He was a talented public speaker and campaigned throughout northern New York for the Republican Party. Within weeks after Lincoln's inauguration, James Nye was appointed governor of the new territory of Nevada.

Traveling west by way of the Isthmus of Panama, Nye arrived at Carson City in July 1861. He lost no time putting the new government in working order. Within three days after his arrival, he proclaimed the organization of the territory complete and announced its officers.

The same month, he ordered a census taken to determine voting districts for seats in the legislature, then ordered the election of members and set the date for its first session. The first bill Nye signed was one adopting the common law, which laid a firm foundation upon which Nevada's future laws were built.

Nye's real talent as a leader was in unifying the people to support the government so it functioned smoothly. His political abilities were later described by Mark Twain, who wrote of him:

He . . . in his early days . . . had acquired the habit of remembering names and faces and making himself agreeable. . . . As a politician this had been valuable to him and he kept his arts in good condition by practice. By the time he had been Governor for a year he had shaken hands with every human being in the Territory of Nevada, and after that he always knew these people instantly by sight and could call them by name. The whole population of 20,000 persons were his personal friends and he could do anything he chose to do and count upon their being contented with it.

During the whole time he was territorial governor, Nye had to contend with the Civil War problems that affected Nevada as well as the rest of the nation. Bringing men of conflicting views together to establish a firm government in a raw new land where heated passion often broke into stormy quarrels was far from easy. The silver boom added to his troubles.

It was hard to raise funds to keep the government going, hard to cope with the incoming rush of fortune seekers, the land claims of settlers and the fact that the population was multiplying every day so that its total doubled in four years. Nye proved himself an able executive. He had the courage to make needed decisions and to stand by them.

From his first moment in office, he worked toward the goal of statehood for Nevada, leading the territorial government to it step by step. The second legislature of 1862 passed an act to frame a constitution for "the state of Washoe." Nye signed it in December and called for an election of delegates the following September.

When the delegates met, they changed the proposed name of the state from Washoe to Nevada, after considering other names for it, such as Humboldt or Esmeralda. For thirty-two days, the delegates argued over seeking admission as a state and most of them were in favor of it. But the voters in the mining districts turned down the move because of a revenue law which would have taxed the mines heavily.

The last session of the territorial legislature was held during the winter of 1864 and President Lincoln signed an act the next March "to enable the people of the Territory of Nevada to form a Constitution and State Government and for the admission of such State into the Union." The act provided that Nevada would be a state when its people ratified a constitution, with no further approval or other action required by Congress.

Delegates who met for the second convention at Carson City in July 1864 used the first constitution as a model, but changed the tax on the mines. A doctor, two editors, miners, farmers, and eleven lawyers were in the group that had come to Nevada mostly from California and New York. They ranged in age from young men in their twenties to old prospectors in their sixties.

Some still objected to statehood, mainly on the grounds that it would cost too much. But those who argued for it won the convention over by calling for faith in the future of the mining industry, in the coming railroads, and for the need of loyalty to the national government that would require Nevada's support during the reconstruction years after the Civil War.

With the constitution ready to be offered to the people, the need was for a man like Nye who could pull together the feelings of the scattered, rootless, silver-hungry population. He made shrewd use of what Mark Twain described as his "winningly friendly face and deep lustrous brown eyes" that could "outtalk his tongue." As a speaker, according to Twain, he could arouse "every feeling, every passion, every emotion."

The people enthusiastically voted for statehood and sent President Lincoln the telegram that announced their decision. Nye carried on his duties as governor for the first five weeks after Nevada became a state, until a general election was held to choose state officers in November.

He moved from the governor's chair to the United States Senate, where he served until 1873. In the Senate, as spokesman for his new state, he was a figure of dignity and elegance, silver-haired and still silver-voiced. He died at White Plains, in his home state of New York, where he had gone for a visit, in December 1876.

NEBRASKA

Motto: Equality Before the Law

Flower: Goldenrod   Bird: Western Meadow Lark

Tree: American Elm

Admitted to the Union: 1867

☆

The Indian Country, which ran from Texas to Canada and from the Missouri border to the Rocky Mountains, was the only unorganized part of the United States after the Missouri Compromise of 1850 was put into effect. It stood as a barrier to the growth of the railroads and to the westward push of settlers, who started moving into the area despite the treaties that reserved the land for the Indians.

Railroads began making surveys and those who wanted to settle began demanding that the Indians give up some of the land. But the whole question of creating a new territory was clouded over by the national issue of whether to allow slavery.

In 1853 Abelard Guthrie was sent as a delegate to Congress by the Wyandotte Indian tribe to urge admission of Nebraska as a territory. Proslavery and antislavery settlers also elected delegates. All three were refused seats in Congress, but a bill to create Nebraska Territory did pass the Senate, although it failed in the House.

Senator Stephen Douglas of Illinois, the home state of the railroad interests, then proposed the Kansas-Nebraska Bill to set up two separate territories. Douglas expected to please both the North and South by giving each side a chance to gain a future state, and thus perhaps become elected President. But the move brought the whole slavery question into angry debate as the great national political issue, and the new Republican Party was born.

Although the Kansas-Nebraska Bill was a total failure as a means of settling the slavery question, it did open the way for the coming railroad to the Pacific. Passed by Congress after five months of stormy quarreling, it created the Territory of Nebraska on May 30, 1854.

Ten years later, Congress approved an act to permit Nebraska to become a state whenever the people were ready for it, but the struggle to achieve a place in the Union wasn't settled until 1867.

TURNER MARQUETT
(1829–1894)

Turner Marquett never wanted to be elected to Congress. He served in Washington as the Representative from Nebraska for only two days, but his election helped make Nebraska a state. For twelve years before that, he had been a leader of the battle for statehood at a time when many Nebraskans fought against joining the Union.

He was a young man in his twenties when he first arrived in Nebraska in 1855, shortly after it had become a territory. Born in Ohio, where his parents were pioneer settlers from Virginia, he hoped to set up a law practice. But clients in the sparsely settled new territory were so few at first that he had to clerk for awhile in a store.

Like many young lawyers, he saw an opportunity to gain a name for himself in politics. Within two years after his arrival, he was elected to the first of seven terms in the territorial legislature. Marquett became an ardent champion of the cause of statehood.

In 1860 the legislature asked the people to vote on adopting a state constitution. The move ran into strong opposition. Much of the area was still unsettled and people were poor.

Opponents argued that taxes were high enough without making a handful of settlers responsible for a state government.

However, President Lincoln wanted Nebraska to become a state so as to strengthen his party's position in Congress during the years that would follow the end of the Civil War. Congress passed an act in 1864 to enable the people to form a constitution and state government. It encouraged them to act by offering large grants of public lands to the new state when it came into being. Once again, the people voted to do nothing about it.

Marquett and the others who favored immediate admission as a state refused to let the matter drop. The next session of the legislature acted on its own to appoint a committee to draft a constitution. It then approved the document by resolution and called for a June election to adopt or reject it and also to choose officials for new state government if Nebraska voted to become a state.

The election battle centered upon Cass County, where people were almost solidly against statehood. Marquett lived in Cass County and it was felt that if he were nominated for Congress, the county residents would vote for him out of local pride and thus carry the state.

"I instructed my friends not to put forward my name," he recalled in later years, "but my nomination, without my consent and against my will, was made. It had the desired effect. Local county pride caused the people of Cass County to vote for state, which they would not have done otherwise, and it was the turning pivot that carried the vote for the state."

When the returns were counted, the constitution had been adopted by a margin of barely two hundred votes. There were many contested seats in the legislature and charges of vote fraud. Those against statehood still hadn't given up. They hoped to influence enough of the newly elected legislators so that no final approval of statehood would be given.

The legislature met in the capitol building in Omaha on the Fourth of July, 1866, and feelings ran high. The plan of the statehood opponents was to get the legislature to adjourn as soon as it met. That would have left the whole issue up in the air and destroyed the work of months in the few minutes it took to call the roll.

Once again, Marquett's Cass County was the center of the dispute. The county's lawmakers held a secret meeting, in which they agreed to vote as a unit against statehood. When the state senate held its first session the next morning, adjournment was quickly voted. It looked as though the state would die without ever having been born.

But Marquett's group went to work on the House members from Cass County. Several of them broke away from the unit vote. Finally, by a single vote, the legislature continued its session. It then went ahead with its business of organizing the government.

Still, the struggle for statehood had not been won. The action moved to Washington where Marquett, Nebraska's new Congressman, and the state's two Senators appeared with their credentials and asked for their seats in the government. A bill to admit Nebraska was introduced in both houses and was passed by a narrow vote.

Congress then adjourned and President Andrew Johnson pocketed the bill, which ended any decision until the next session. Between sessions, Johnson took a stand against Nebraska as part of his general policy on the matter of state versus federal rights. Meanwhile, Marquett and Nebraska's Senators had to return home to face another state election in October. Marquett thus had to run for Congress twice within four months. He carried the re-election by only several hundred votes.

Nebraska's sole hope of achieving federal approval for statehood lay in getting a two-thirds majority in Congress to pass the bill against Johnson's veto. The vote of the Senate seemed fairly certain, but there was grave doubt that the House would approve. Marquett appealed for help to Ohio's Representative Shellabarger, who had been his instructor when Marquett was going to law school.

"It so happened that he and I were from the same county in Ohio and I knew him before I came west," Marquett said later. "I renewed the acquaintance and I think this had its influence."

Shellabarger was one of the most prominent and respected members of the House and an eloquent speaker. He took the lead in championing the Nebraska statehood bill and made a speech of great force and brilliance. It had a deciding effect and the bill won House approval. When President Johnson vetoed it as expected the next day, it was passed over his head by a majority of both houses.

Nebraska's state legislature met to approve certain changes in the wording of the constitution that Congress had asked and, on March 1, President Johnson was forced to recognize Nebraska's admission to the Union.

The current session of Congress was about to end and by waiting two more days to apply for his seat in it, Marquett could have served as Nebraska's first Congressman for a full term. But he had fought so hard and so long to have Nebraska become a state that he wanted to present his credentials at once and make statehood final.

"I deemed it but right under the circumstances to go in and have myself sworn in for two days and out for two years," he said. "Many thought it a foolish act, yet I would do the same thing again. I ran twice for Congress in one year, was elected both times, and served two days and really two nights, but I never charged anything for that."

Weary of politics, with the goal of statehood at last achieved, Marquett retired from office to devote his full time to law. He became one of the most expert and distinguished corporation lawyers in the West. For the last twenty years of his life, he represented the railroads which soon brought their tracks across the land he had helped to make the state of Nebraska.

PART V. THE SECOND CENTURY

COLORADO

Motto: Nothing Without Providence
Flower: Rocky Mountain Columbine   Bird: Lark Bunting
Tree: Colorado Blue Spruce
Admitted to the Union: 1876

☆

Colorado, the Centennial State, was admitted to the Union one hundred years after the Declaration of Independence.

There was nothing to attract settlement to the area until gold was discovered in 1858. The cry of "Pikes Peak or Bust" swept the East and brought the first of the Argonauts that same year. Within two years, a dozen cities were established in what had been an uninhabited part of Kansas Territory.

Early in 1860 the first move for statehood began, but a proposed constitution was rejected by the people. Later that year, a territorial constitution was ratified. People's courts and miners' courts were established as a local form of government to control the booming settlements.

Colorado became accepted by Congress as an independent territory in 1861. Six years later it was ready for statehood, but the act that would have enabled it to become a state was vetoed by President Johnson. After nearly a decade more of seeking a place in the Union, statehood finally was granted on August 1, 1876.

JOHN EVANS

(*1814–1897*)

John Evans was a man of many careers who rose to prominence in three different states.

As a physician, he first gained fame in Indiana. Moving to Illinois, he helped to found Northwestern University. He came to Colorado as the appointed governor of the territory and remained to build its railroads, its university and establish many of its churches. Doctor, educator, business magnate and champion of statehood, he was chosen by the people to become a first Senator from Colorado, but never gained his seat in the Senate.

Born in 1814 in Ohio, the son of a moderately wealthy Quaker farmer and storekeeper, he quarreled with his parents over his desire to become a doctor. They were so set against his choice of a career that they refused to help him, but he managed to borrow enough money from friends to enter a medical college in Cincinnati.

He was twenty-four when he graduated, and decided the same year to get married. Evans and his bride moved to Indiana, where he started his medical practice and also became interested in business to the extent of building a block of stores and offices that added to his income. He took the lead in a campaign to have the state establish its first hospital for the insane and moved to Indianapolis as its superintendent.

Although still only a young man, he soon achieved such standing in medical circles that he was invited to become a professor at Rush Medical College in Chicago. Evans and his family bought a home in the outskirts of Chicago, and the suburb where he lived later took his name and became Evanston. In addition to teaching, he was editor and part owner of a medical journal, helped to found Chicago's Mercy Hospital and was elected a city alderman.

As an educator, he became chairman of Chicago's school committee and a co-founder of Northwestern University. His business interests turned again to real estate and then to railroad investments. By the time he was forty-five, his growing wealth and financial activities made him decide to give up his medical practice.

Three years later, during the Civil War, Evans was appointed territorial governor of Colorado, just one year after it had become a territory. He moved at once to Denver and almost immediately found himself deep in the problems of trying to build a government in an area that had boomed with a rush of gold seekers and had been caught in the troubles of a nation at war.

On the one hand, he had to deal with the threat of rebellious Indians, and on the other, recruit and assemble troops to support the Union. Invading Texans hoped to capture the region for the South. And on the home battlefront of local politics, Colorado's settlers were still quarreling over the issue of statehood that most of them had rejected only a short while before Evans arrived.

A builder by nature and an organizer of men, he took over the leadership of the statehood movement. Largely because of his influence, it gradually regained support. By the time the war was ending, Colorado had high hopes of becoming a state.

In 1863 a statehood bill was introduced in Congress, but never reached the floor for a vote. The next year, an act was passed and a constitution was drawn up and accepted by the people of Colorado. They chose Evans to be one of their first Senators. Congress voted to make Colorado a state.

But he never took office because President Andrew Johnson turned down the statehood bill in 1866 and vetoed another attempt the following year. The action was a personal defeat for Evans as well as a crushing disappointment to the people, and he retired from politics.

Evans' faith in the future growth of Colorado remained unshaken. If he couldn't lead it to immediate statehood, he could help it to grow in other ways that would build a state.

If he was denied the honor of being Colorado's voice in the United States Senate, he could still help to build its commerce, its business, its civic and cultural institutions that would bring increased settlement.

Railroads meant growth in those years and when it became known that Denver would not be on the line of the new railroad being built across the continent, Evans organized a company that built a railroad to connect Denver with the Union Pacific at Cheyenne.

However, after the company was established it ran into financial troubles and was about to fail. Evans personally took upon himself complete responsibility for the line that would rescue Denver from isolation. When it was completed in 1870 he was acclaimed a hero by the people, who cheered the first run over the new tracks. He later helped to establish another railroad that crossed the mountains to the mining country and a third that connected Denver with the South.

During the years Colorado was waiting to be admitted as a state, Evans contributed to the building of dozens of churches, helped to found the college that later became the University of Denver and was its main financial support, and increased his own wealth as well as that of Colorado by backing scores of business ventures and financing the construction of blocks of buildings.

Meanwhile another convention met in Denver in 1875 to draft another constitution. It was ratified by the people and, at last, Congress admitted Colorado as the thirty-eighth state. Evans was in his sixties by then, but he was nearly eighty before he completely retired from his active life.

In 1895, by an act of the legislature, the mountain peak west of Denver was renamed Mount Evans in his honor. When he died at the age of eighty-three in 1897, enormous crowds turned out for his state funeral. It was on the third of July, one day before Colorado celebrated the anniversary of the nation's independence and its own twenty-first anniversary of statehood.

NORTH DAKOTA

Motto: Liberty and Union, Now and
Forever, One and Inseparable

Flower: Prairie Rose   Bird: Western Meadow Lark

Tree: Elm

Admitted to the Union: 1889

☆

When Dakota Territory was organized in 1861, President
Lincoln appointed his family doctor, William Jane, as its first
governor. In the twenty-eight years it remained a territory,
other governors came and left so rapidly that one official
wrote: "A boy could play marbles on their flying coat tails."

Nearly all the appointed territorial high officials were from
the East and most of them were extremely unpopular with the
people. But politics were hotly fought on the local level, too,
with nighttime raids to capture county voting records and occasional gunplay to punctuate oratory of would-be candidates.
It was a time when self-seeking politicians often indulged in
high-handed trickery to satisfy their own ambitions.

The northern and southern parts of the territory had little
in common and they kept growing farther apart. Settlement
was slow and the northern section didn't really begin to develop until about 1874 when the Northern Pacific Railroad
was built as far as Bismarck on the Missouri River. In five
years the railroad doubled the region's population.

Railroad interests practically controlled North Dakota's
early government, but the railroads also helped the area grow
to statehood. Immigrants found it easier to reach government
lands by rail and were encouraged to settle so as to increase
railroad business.

Great model farms were established, with farming methods more modern than those used in the East, and stories of their fabulous crops were spread by railroad colonizing agents in Europe as well as in America. Low fares, emigrant guide-books, and widespread publicity soon drew settlers by the hundreds.

The legislature of 1871 first asked Congress to divide the territory. Three years later, a petition was introduced to make the northern part a separate territory named Pembina. Nearly every year after that, Congress was asked to admit two states instead of one. In 1880 it was suggested that the northern part be called North Dakota.

The real break between the two sections came after the removal of the territorial capital to Bismarck in 1883. Two years later, the southern area tried to move it to Pierre, but the attempt failed. Sentiment for forming two separate states grew, but Congress, which was Democratic at the time, didn't relish the idea of admitting four new Republican Senators.

An enabling act finally was passed in 1889 and North Dakota delegates who met that year at a constitutional convention produced a document six times as long as the Federal Constitution. Republican President Benjamin Harrison signed the proclamations making both North and South Dakota states. The proclamations were covered with sheets of newspaper so that neither Harrison nor anybody else would know which one he was signing first. That is why, to this day, nobody can say whether North Dakota or South Dakota was the nation's thirty-ninth state.

BURLEIGH SPALDING
(1853–1934)

Burleigh Spalding was in his late twenties in 1880 when he arrived in Fargo, Dakota Territory, to practice law. Born in Vermont, he had worked on farms, taught school and sold books from door to door to pay his way through college. He also had learned something of politics, serving as a clerk to the Vermont legislature.

Like many other Easterners seeking opportunity in a booming new territory, he had been lured to Dakota by those who sang the praises of Fargo as the gateway to a new "promised land." Fargo was where the busy river steamboats and the new railroad met, the stepping-off place for the thousands of settlers who were to come to the frontier, and was a supply center for the great new wheat farms.

Ten years before, it had been Indian country, virgin prairie land, but by the time Spalding arrived in 1880, Fargo already was changing from a frontier village to a city. Nearly three thousand people had settled the town and there were imposing stone buildings, hotels, a concert hall, a daily newspaper and a school. Farmers in slouch hats, lumberers in red flannel jackets, Indians, merchants, even other lawyers such as he, crowded the busy main street where light horse-drawn buggies hurried past the heavy freight wagons drawn by teams of oxen.

In such a place, at such a time, a man who knew his way around in matters of politics and government quickly found himself looked up to for leadership by those who hoped to make North Dakota a state separate from the territory to the south. He was welcomed at the new three-story combined hotel and railroad depot, the social center of Fargo, which had just been rebuilt by the town's progressive businessmen after a disastrous fire had destroyed the original building.

Visible for miles on the flat prairie, it was the landmark around which flowed the life and business of frontier Fargo. There and in the gray frame Cass County courthouse where he argued his cases, Spalding became a prominent and well-liked young man. The political bosses were the men who served the interests of the railroad, and it wasn't long before he was chosen for an important part in their plan to move the territorial capital.

The northern and southern sections of the territory were already moving apart in sentiment. There had been meetings and much discussion over dividing Dakota into two territories and eventually into two states. The legislature had been seeking a division. But no direct action had been taken.

Yankton, on the Missouri River at the extreme southern border, was still the territorial capital in 1883. Naturally, the citizens of Yankton wanted to keep it there. But the political group of which Spalding had become a leading figure managed to get the legislature to create a committee of nine commissioners to choose a capital city.

Spalding was named to represent Cass County. According to the law, the commissioners had to meet and organize at Yankton before they looked at any of the other sites. People in Yankton believed the act was illegal. They planned to get a court order to hold the commissioners there while the entire issue was fought out. In that way, they expected to delay things long enough to keep the capital.

Armed with a court order, they waited for the commissioners to start their meeting. But, unknown to the citizens of Yankton, Spalding and the rest of the commissioners had chartered a special train. It left Sioux City at three o'clock in the morning. The coach in which the commissioners sat was dimly lighted as the train pulled into the city limits of Yankton. The train didn't stop there at all. Instead, it slowly kept on moving. While it moved, the commissioners quickly called a meeting aboard it. They chose Spalding secretary of the group, elected other officers, and then adjourned.

Having met, organized and adjourned in Yankton, the commissioners satisfied the law and kept the court from interfering. When the meeting finished, the train still had half a mile to go before it passed beyond Yankton's city limits.

Yankton raised a great cry of having been tricked, but the plan worked. Spalding and the rest of the commissioners made a grand tour of all the prospective capital sites. They were royally entertained, wined and dined in each of the cities, which offered up to $100,000 and various amounts of land to be selected. After looking over the different places and enjoying the hospitality, the commissioners held a meeting in

Spalding's Fargo and chose Bismarck as the new capital of the territory.

Yankton took the matter into court, but meanwhile the cornerstone of the new capitol building was laid at Bismarck at elaborate ceremonies attended by famous national leaders and foreign dignitaries who were on their way west to celebrate the Golden Spike completion of the Northern Pacific Railroad. The guests were headed by ex-President Grant and the cornerstone ceremony touched off a land boom that sent Bismarck's real estate values skyrocketing.

Dakota's next territorial governor, Gilbert Pierce, moved the capital there and the legislature met in Bismarck in 1885. People in the southern part of the territory, brought to the point of an open break with those in the north, got the legislature to pass a bill to move the capital from Bismarck to Pierre. But Governor Pierce vetoed it. He upheld the action of Spalding's committee in choosing Bismarck.

This created strong feeling between the two sections as Dakota moved toward statehood. Spalding became Cass County's superintendent of schools. But, while that was his official job, he spent much time working behind the scenes on the political developments soon to take place.

In 1885 a constitutional convention was held in Sioux Falls, a constitution adopted, and Congress was asked to create two states. Because of the national political situation, Dakota being Republican and Congress Democratic, no action was taken. Spalding had become a Republican leader of the North Dakotan group and when Republican Benjamin Harrison finally became President, enabling bills were passed allowing for separate statehood for North and South Dakota.

Spalding was chosen a member of the convention that framed the North Dakota convention of 1889. He and the rest of the writers of the constitution met at Bismarck on July 4th and were entertained by a parade in which Sitting Bull and other famous, and by then peaceful, Indians took part. By August 17th, North Dakota's lengthy constitution was complete.

The people voted to accept it and President Harrison proclaimed North Dakota a state. Spalding went on to become chairman of the State Republican committee, was elected to two terms in Congress, twice was made a state court justice and finally, in 1911, became chief justice of North Dakota's supreme court.

SOUTH DAKOTA

Motto: Under God, the People Rule

Flower: Pasqueflower   Bird: Ring-necked Pheasant

Tree: Black Hills Spruce

Admitted to the Union: 1889

☆

When men of General George Custer's military command discovered gold in the Black Hills in 1874, it started a rush of
gold seekers into what had been Indian lands. New discoveries
brought 25,000 people into Deadwood Gulch by the summer
of 1876.

Many people who came to look for gold remained to take
up farms. Meanwhile, the growth of the railroads brought a
fresh flood of settlers and a great land boom to the area. Much
of South Dakota was settled in the twelve years just before
statehood. There were only sixty miles of railroad tracks in the
territory in 1878, but less than ten years later more than a
thousand miles of railroads had been built.

People in the northern and the southern parts of the Dakota Territory had different interests and the move toward
creating two separate states grew with the increase in population. After the politicians in the northern section moved the
state capital out of the southern area, there were several attempts to make a state of South Dakota.

The national government refused to permit the entry of
two states instead of one until Benjamin Harrison made the
admission a campaign issue in 1888 in his successful bid for
the Presidency.

When Dakota first became a territory, which included both
the present states as well as parts of Montana and Wyoming,

the total non-Indian population in the vast land area was less than 2,500. By the time South Dakota gained admission as a state, the boom had brought in 300,000 settlers.

ARTHUR MELLETTE
(1842–1896)

Arthur Mellette gave everything he had to the state of South Dakota.

During the years when the Federal Government wanted to make one state of the Dakota Territory, he led South Dakota to separate statehood. He served as provisional governor, territorial governor and state governor.

After Mellette retired, he turned over all his property to the state in an attempt to repay the money taken by his state treasurer who made off with public funds.

One of Mellette's ancestors was a French soldier who came to America to fight in the Revolution and stayed to settle in Virginia. Mellette himself was born on an Indiana farm his father had homesteaded. Although there wasn't much chance for him to go to school as a boy, he had a thirst for learning and was able to teach himself well enough to enter Indiana University.

He was twenty-two when he graduated in 1864. During the Civil War he was an army private, but decided to return to the university after the war to become a lawyer. After he was admitted to the bar, he married Margaret Wylie and settled down to practice law in Muncie. There he became interested in journalism and in politics. A newspaper job led to his election to the Indiana legislature.

Remembering how hard it was for him as a farm boy to get a good education, Mellette devised a township school system that was adopted by Indiana and became a model for the educational programs in several other states as well. He had begun to win a promising future for himself in Indiana politics when his wife became ill. Doctors prescribed a change in climate.

Mellette gave up his law practice and what he thought was his political future, disposed of his home and all his business interests, and moved with her to Dakota Territory. He was able to obtain an appointment as a federal land office agent for awhile, until he could establish a new law practice in Watertown. By then Mellette was a man of forty, but instead of being ended, his real career in politics had just started.

His neighbors and friends were seeking separate statehood for the southern part of Dakota Territory and Mellette soon became a leader of the movement. In 1882 the legislature passed a bill calling for a constitutional convention. When it was vetoed by Nehemiah Ordway, the man then serving as Dakota's appointed governor, the committee representing the southern part of the territory went ahead on its own and called for a convention of delegates to meet the following June.

Delegates from every county in South Dakota met at Huron and decided to hold a constitutional convention in Sioux Falls in September. Mellette, chosen as one of the members of that convention, helped to write parts of the first proposed constitution and some of his suggestions were carried over into the later versions of it. When the constitution was put before the people, they voted for it almost unanimously.

It was presented to Congress, along with a petition for statehood, but Congress refused to act. Another constitution was framed and once more ratified by the people in 1885. But the Democratic national administration was against any plan that would admit four new Republican Senators and cut down the Democratic majority in the United States Senate. The Democratic leaders favored admitting the whole territory as a single state.

Mellette refused to give in to the Federal Government. He held out for separate statehood for South Dakota. Under his leadership, the South Dakotans held an election. They elected a legislature, selected Mellette as provisional governor, chose

Huron as their capital, and claimed that South Dakota existed, in fact, as a state.

He pointed out that Michigan previously had taken somewhat the same action and that since Congress had granted recognition to Michigan, a sound precedent had been set. When Congress still refused to recognize Mellette's self-proclaimed state, he determined to work for a change in national administration and the election of a President who would approve statehood.

Mellette used all his political influence to support Benjamin Harrison in the Dakota Territory and also helped to win many votes for him in neighboring states. The Republicans made a campaign issue of two states, instead of one, for the Dakotas. Harrison's election brought Congressional passage of an enabling act. One of Harrison's first appointments after he was inaugurated President was Arthur Mellette as governor of Dakota Territory.

As territorial governor, Mellette promptly issued the call for another constitutional convention in the summer of 1889, with power only to amend and resubmit the previous constitution to the people. South Dakotans approved it on October 1st. One month later, Mellette's long fight ended with President Harrison's proclamation admitting both North and South Dakota to the Union.

In the first election, the people chose Mellette governor of their new state. He worked hard to set up a state government that would be a model for those who followed him, and especially to keep down the cost of it. When his health began to fail in 1893 he retired from the governorship to take up his private law practice again in Watertown.

His hilltop home was a showplace that reflected the style of the period, a three-story house that offered a view of the whole countryside for miles around. With block towers and an encircling porch, it had an inside spiral staircase which rose to the crowning cupola, and Mellette was justly proud of it.

With a thirst for knowledge that was as strong in his old age as it had been when he was a boy on an Indiana farm, Mellette planned to devote his last years to the study of physics. He hoped to build a laboratory in his home and equip it with money he had saved through the years.

But it wasn't long after he retired before a scandal broke. The man who had been state treasurer during Mellette's governorship was accused of running off with most of the state funds. Although he wasn't personally to blame, Mellette turned over his fine home, his entire fortune, and everything else he owned to the state.

He gave up his dream of an old age of study and research and went to spend his last days with one of his children in Kansas. The old house had many tenants after Mellette died in 1896. All the furnishings and even the doors and windows were removed. For a time it served, among other things, as the studio of a radio station. Finally the decaying building was condemned.

In 1943 it was bought by a civic association and funds were raised to restore and refurnish it, so it once again would be the showplace it had been in Mellette's time, to serve the memory of South Dakota's state maker.

MONTANA

Motto: Gold and Silver

Flower: Bitterroot   Bird: Western Meadow Lark

Tree: Ponderosa Pine

Admitted to the Union: 1889

☆

The part of the country that became Montana was pretty much a neglected wilderness for years. After the early fur-trapping days ended, a military road was built through the area, but it had few travelers. The Indians made the land too dangerous for settlement and there was nothing to attract people to the region until gold and then other mineral riches were discovered.

Even the fear of Indians could not keep out the great rush of miners and prospectors. There was little law and order of any kind in some of the mining camps that sprang up during the boom years. They were miles away from the nearest centers of legal government. Montana was made a separate territory in 1864 largely to bring some form of federal control to the scattered mining settlements where rough-and-ready frontier justice was the rule.

Copper became even more of a lure than gold and the discovery of some of the world's richest copper deposits led to a long battle among big mining interests that dominated local politics. The copper kings feuded among themselves, bossed the camps and towns, ran the government. Miners began to organize unions to break the hold of the copper companies and also to seek political power.

Outside the mining towns, the Indians still ruled the plains. It wasn't until after the Indians were subdued that ranchers and rural settlers arrived in great numbers. Montana waited twenty-five years after it became a territory before it gained statehood in 1889.

JOSEPH TOOLE
(1851–1928)

Joseph Toole and his older brother, Edwin, worked together to bring law and orderly government to Montana. Edwin fought in the courts to help create what amounted to a code of law in nearly lawless mining towns of the frontier. Joseph battled in the halls of government to win statehood for Montana and then to lead the new state through its forming years.

From the time he was in his teens, Joseph Toole wanted to be a lawyer like his brother Edwin. Born in Missouri in 1851, the youngest of eight brothers and sisters, Joseph went to school in St. Joseph and then to a military institute for boys in Kentucky. When he graduated at the age of seventeen, he worked in a law office to study for his bar examinations.

About a year later, Edwin sent for him to come West. Edwin had left his own law practice in Missouri to adventure into the Far West, journeying to Colorado, then Idaho, and finally settling in Virginia City, Montana. He found there was practically no law at all in the booming mine camp.

With the consent of the miners, he established a crude system of laws. Soon other camps called upon him for legal help. Although he held no official position, since there was no real local government, Edwin began traveling from one camp to another, arguing cases in hastily assembled courts.

His reasoning and legal logic helped persuade the various communities to accept his opinions. Because of his influence, the local courts in the area grew more orderly and were more in general agreement as to what the basic mine camp laws should be.

Edwin Toole moved to Helena in 1865 to establish his law practice there. Four years later, he sent for Joseph, who finished his legal training in Edwin's office and became his partner after he was admitted to the bar. Joseph was keenly interested in politics and he became a leader of Montana's young Democrats.

Serving as district attorney, Joseph furthered his political ambitions and decided in 1881 to run for election to the territorial council. He won the election and immediately was chosen council president. Already a strong supporter of statehood, he succeeded in having a constitutional convention called in 1884, but Congress refused to recognize the constitution that was drafted.

Joseph Toole decided to carry the statehood battle to Washington. Elected to Congress as a territorial delegate in 1885, he devoted nearly four years to winning Congressional approval of a bill that would lead to Montana's admission as a state. He was also an active supporter of the Omnibus Bill of 1889 that provided for the admission of North and South Dakota and Washington as states, as well as Montana.

Chosen a member of the Montana convention of 1889 to frame the state constitution, he fought successfully to include in the document many of its guarantees of social and civil rights.

The people of Montana voted to make Joseph Toole the first governor of the state. Though it was a wealthy new state in terms of its rich mining resources, Toole ran into money problems almost at once. He was faced with a legislature that was politically deadlocked and refused to provide funds for the government. Toole guided Montana through its first year on credit. He steered the state through its political troubles and sent the second legislature an extensive program for organizing a solid state government. His plans included an improved school system.

When his first term as governor was over, he decided to take time out to join his brother once more in private law practice. One of the big cases they worked on together resulted in a decision against a railroad that claimed mining rights to land granted for building tracks. The Toole brothers kept more than 75,000 square miles of rich mineral lands for the state. Together, they also helped to win the fight to have Montana's capital permanently located at Helena.

Twice more, in 1900 and again in 1904, Joseph Toole was elected governor. After his brother Edwin died, Joseph resigned the governorship in 1908 because of his own ill health. He retired to California, where he lived another twenty years. Although he was outside the state, he still had an influence upon its affairs. His opinions often were sought by those who developed the government he had helped create.

WASHINGTON

Motto: Al-Ki (Indian word meaning Bye and Bye)

Flower: Rhododendron   Bird: Goldfinch

Tree: Hemlock

Admitted to the Union: 1889

☆

There was no permanent American settlement in Washington until 1845, when Tumwater was established on Puget Sound as the western end of the Oregon Trail. Washington, first a part of Oregon, became a separate territory in 1853. Settlers were slow to come to the land north of the Columbia River because of the Indians.

The first territorial governor, Isaac Stevens, made many treaties with them, but trouble with the Indians went on for more than thirty years. Mining discoveries brought in flurries of hopeful prospectors who had been disappointed in the earlier gold and silver rushes in nearby states. However, farmers, townspeople and other home-making settlers did not come to Washington in any great numbers until after the railroads crisscrossed the region. Then, in the ten years from 1880 to 1890, the population grew to nearly four times what it had been before.

Congress turned down a number of early bids that Washington made for statehood. State-making hopes led to holding a constitutional convention in 1878. But it wasn't until eleven years later, in 1889, that statehood was granted, and it was the convention held that same year that framed the constitution accepted by the voters and finally approved by Congress.

WATSON SQUIRE
(*1838–1926*)

When the delegates met at Ellensburg on the Fourth of July in 1889 to write a constitution for what was to become the state of Washington, the man they chose to preside over their convention was Watson Squire. He had been governor of the territory during its unruly boom years. But, more importantly, Squire had been a supersalesman.

His sales ability and his own faith in the future of the area helped to convince Eastern bankers and financiers to invest in the railroads, mines and industries of what was a near wilderness. As a businessman, even more than as a politician, Squire sold them the idea of developing Washington. He encouraged the sudden flourishing growth that brought in enough settlers in ten years to form a stable government and create a state.

Squire, born a minister's son in upstate New York, became a schoolteacher and then turned to the study of law just before the outbreak of the Civil War. During the war, he enlisted as a private and rose to captain a company serving on the Western frontier, and then to become a judge advocate and a colonel.

When the war ended he looked around for a job and finally took one as a salesman with a leading munitions firm which had sold weapons to the Union Army. The company was seeking new sales outlets for its firearms, as well as other lines of business to replace its wartime production of guns. Squire's salesmanship soon made him a company executive. When he was thirty he married the owner's daughter, Ida Remington.

His sales trips took him all over Europe and to Mexico. During the Franco-Prussian War, he arranged the sale of weapons to France. Entertained by rulers, diplomats and the top men of the business world, Squire made important friendships with those who had money to invest in new enterprises.

It was after the glamour of Europe and the high society of New York and other Eastern cities that he had his first view of Washington Territory's Puget Sound area in 1879. Seattle was then a village of only about three thousand people. Its muddy streets were unpaved and the sidewalks were planked wood, but the main street did boast of new gas lighting.

Squire arrived as a salesman, to look over the area as a place where the sale of firearms might be boosted. He found plenty of guns being used in the rough waterfront town, where street brawls and even shootings were common and where the smuggling of goods and of men, the hijacking of cargoes and the shanghaiing of sailors were not unusual in those lawless days.

He also saw the booming harbor activity of a port serving more than a hundred regular ships of trade, the businesses and new industries springing up at every hand, and he had the vision to look to the future metropolis that might grow there and the state that might be. There was much more to be built than a stronger sales territory for firearms. He decided Seattle was to be his home, and his excitement over the possibilities it offered soon was a part of the letters he was writing East.

The bankers and financiers Squire knew were a whole continent away, but his own faith in Washington's future encouraged them to invest in the ventures that quickened the boom. Squire also understood the need for good government, for Washington's acceptance as a state, and used his influence with men of position to gain the political support that would ease the move toward statehood.

He built an opera house, invested his own funds in vast real estate holdings, increased his personal wealth, and became a respected leader of territorial affairs. In 1884 President Chester Arthur named Watson Squire governor of the territory. Squire served as governor for three years.

They were troubled years of unrest, of lingering lawlessness, of almost bursting growth in population, a time of labor riots and of racial troubles involving large numbers of Chinese brought in as workers. Squire's firmness in maintaining law and in restoring order to riot-torn sections of the mush-rooming city added to his personal popularity and also helped to reassure those investing in business and industry.

He resigned the governorship to devote himself to his private affairs, but the voters called upon him to take the lead once more as Washington neared the climax of its bid for statehood. On July 4, 1889, Squire called to order the first session of the constitutional convention. Within seven weeks, he had guided the seventy-five delegates into an agreement on the wording of the constitution.

It was approved by the voters the following October and, at the first meeting of the state legislature, Squire was elected to represent the new state in the United States Senate. When his short initial term expired, the people re-elected him Senator and he continued in office until 1897.

During his terms as Senator, he constantly fought for measures that would increase the development of Washington's mineral resources, harbors and rivers, and for projects such as the planned Panama Canal to boost West Coast trade.

Squire was fifty-nine when he quit the Senate. For nearly thirty years more, he took an active part in the business and finance of Washington State. When he died in 1926 at the age of eighty-eight, more than half his life had been devoted to the state his salesmanship and leadership had helped to build and to grow.

IDAHO

Motto: Exist Forever

Flower: Mock Orange   Bird: Mountain Bluebird

Tree: White Pine

Admitted to the Union: 1890

☆

Idaho was part of Oregon and then of Washington before it became a separate territory in 1863. The original Idaho Territory included Wyoming, Montana, and parts of Nebraska and the Dakotas. It took in a land area bigger than Texas.

During the days before it was a territory, both British and American fur traders roamed the region and some of them set up trading posts. Idaho was crossed by covered wagons headed for Oregon, Washington and northern California, and the army established forts to protect travelers from the Indians.

But Idaho's first permanent settlement was made in 1860 at Franklin by some Mormons who thought they were still in Utah. That was the same year gold was discovered. Miners and prospectors flooded into the Idaho gold fields, hoping to strike it rich, but most of them didn't care how or by whom they were governed.

Idaho was made a territory in an attempt to bring some form of law and order to the frequently wild and rowdy mine towns that boomed into existence almost overnight. But some of the men appointed as governors of the new territory never arrived to take their positions. Others used the governorship to promote their own interests or to fatten their purses with money from the public treasury.

The population continued to grow as new discoveries of

gold and silver were made. Gradually, after the Indians were brought under control, the rich grazing lands attracted cattle and sheep growers who began to develop ranches in the valleys. Farmers and town settlers also moved in. For years, however, there were vast mining areas that remained almost without law and with little interest in seeking a state government.

In 1884, only six years before statehood, the discovery of fabulously rich lead and silver deposits at Coeur d'Alene caused a stampede of men into the area that was even wilder than some of the earlier gold rushes. Meanwhile, the more orderly citizens had begun their serious efforts to bring state government to Idaho and admission finally was granted in 1890.

GEORGE SHOUP
(1836–1904)

George Shoup was in his teens when he set out to strike it rich in the gold fields of the West. He was a man of thirty by the time he wandered into Idaho in 1866. By then, he had decided there was more money to be made in business than by trying to dig wealth out of the ground.

Behind him was a life of adventure that included one attempt at making a state. He realized that business prosperity depended upon orderly government. So, he tried again to help guide an unruly and sometimes lawless territory to statehood. And in Idaho he succeeded.

Born in Pennsylvania, he moved with his parents to Illinois when he was sixteen. The Shoups had hardly settled in their new home when the financial panic of 1857 paralyzed the nation's business and left the family nearly penniless.

When he heard the news that gold had been discovered in Colorado, young George set out on his own to try to recoup the family's fortune. He was among the first of the Argonauts to arrive at the gold fields near Pikes Peak. In order to support himself while he was hopefully prospecting for gold, he took along a small stock of merchandise he could sell to other miners for ready cash.

As a miner, he failed to strike it rich. But as a merchant, he grew more successful. He was a popular young man, already the sort that others looked to for leadership, and he began to take an active part in the campaign to win statehood for Colorado. The outbreak of the Civil War interrupted.

He enlisted with a company of independent scouts that patrolled a wide area from Colorado to New Mexico and Texas. When the Third Colorado Cavalry was formed, George Shoup became its colonel and bravely led his men in action.

But his part in Colorado's bid for statehood was recognized as so important he was given a leave of absence from the army in 1864 to attend the convention of delegates meeting to write a proposed constitution. Although it was accepted by Colorado's voters, and also by Congress, President Andrew Johnson turned down the statehood bill.

When the war ended, Shoup decided to move on from Colorado to the new mining camps in Montana. There were high profits to be made there as a merchant, and he took his own stock of goods with him and opened a store near Montana's Virginia City early in 1866. Before the year was over, he decided to move again, still following the gold rushes, but as a merchant, not as a prospector.

He moved his merchandise a hundred miles to the west and helped to found the town of Salmon in the new territory of Idaho, which was to become his permanent home. His business ventures prospered and he married and began a new political career when he was chosen a commissioner to help organize the county government.

Elected to the territorial legislature, Shoup next became a member of the territory's governing council. He also served as Idaho's member of the National Committee of the Republican Party. As his political influence grew, Shoup took upon himself the task of making the entire nation aware of Idaho's right to a place in the Union.

In 1884 New Orleans held a great celebration, a trade fair called the Cotton Centennial. Shoup represented Idaho at the exposition and spent thousands of dollars of his own money to advertise Idaho's resources to the world. Wherever he went and in whatever way he could, he publicized the territory he hoped to make a state.

When Benjamin Harrison appointed Shoup governor of the territory in 1889, he was the sixteenth man who had been named its chief executive. Many had never really served in Idaho or hadn't stayed long enough to establish good government. Shoup was determined that he would be the last governor of Idaho as a territory. Appointed in April, he called for a constitutional statehood convention to meet in July.

The proposed constitution was approved by the convention delegates and Shoup personally carried it to Washington. He went to work with the territory's representative to Congress, Fred Dubois, to win Congressional approval. For twenty-six years Idaho had been a territory. President Harrison authorized Idaho's admission as a state just one day short of a year from the day the constitutional convention first met.

In the new state's first election, the voters overwhelmingly chose George Shoup their governor. He called the legislature to meet on December 1, 1890. It was the custom then for the legislature to choose a state's Senators. The legislature elected Dubois as one Senator and Governor Shoup as the other. He resigned as governor and left the next month for Washington to take his seat in the Senate.

George Shoup was Idaho's Senator for ten years, until he was defeated for re-election in 1901 when he took a stand against the free silver movement. Three years later, he died in Boise. The state honored his memory by placing a statue of him in the nation's capitol, where it stands in Statuary Hall as a lasting tribute to Idaho's state maker.

WYOMING

Motto: Equal Rights

Flower: Indian Paintbrush   Bird: Meadow Lark

Tree: Cottonwood

Admitted to the Union: 1890

☆

On today's maps, Wyoming is a neat rectangle of a state, but it took some thirty changes of boundary lines to make it that way. Wyoming is made up of lands acquired from France, Britain, Texas and Spain, areas that at one time or another were parts of the territories of Dakota, Nebraska, Utah and Idaho.

Wyoming had its share of fur trappers during the early days, and some 60,000 people traveled across it in 1850 on their way to California and Oregon. However, not many stayed to settle. People didn't linger in Wyoming in any numbers until the arrival of the Union Pacific Railroad in 1867 brought a trail of towns and settlements along the line.

For political reasons, Dakota was glad to give up Wyoming and it became a separate territory in 1868. Great cattle ranches developed after it was learned that it cost almost nothing to keep cattle on the open range until they reached market size. Wyoming cattlemen fought sheep ranchers in some of the bitterest feuds of the West and both groups fought against the farmers who came later to divide the open range into small homesteads.

Soon after Wyoming became a territory, its legislature was the first to give equal rights to women. They served on Wyoming juries in 1870, the year the first woman also was appointed a justice of the peace. But it took twenty years more for Wyoming to become a state.

FRANCIS WARREN
(*1844–1929*)

Francis Warren was a man who thought for himself. He seldom let popular opinion sway his decisions. In Wyoming, where the bad feeling between sheepmen and cattlemen brought open warfare, Warren managed to make both groups like him, and he raised both sheep and cattle. He combined the caution of his New England ancestry with bold daring that made him a hero soldier of the Civil War and a champion of law and order in one of the wildest towns of the Western frontier.

Warren's ancestors were among the earliest New England colonists and he was brought up in the western Massachusetts town of Hinsdale, where he was born in 1844. His parents were frugal people and extremely poor.

When he was a boy, he was forced to leave school to help out at home. But as soon as he could be spared he took a job at a nearby farm and worked his way through Hinsdale Academy. Before he was eighteen he was made manager of the farm where he worked.

The Civil War began just about the time of his eighteenth birthday. Warren enlisted in the Forty-ninth Massachusetts Regiment. Fighting in the South, he was among a group of volunteers who helped prepare the ground for an artillery charge near Port Hudson, Louisiana.

Some of his army companions told him he was foolhardy, that he would never come back alive. But Warren was one of the few survivors of the action and was awarded the Congressional Medal of Honor for "courage above and beyond the call of duty."

After the war, instead of settling down to the farm management work that was waiting for him, he again made his own decision. The West was growing fast and he saw a bright future for himself as a merchant in one of the new boom towns. Traveling across the country, finding a job here or there as the opportunity offered, he reached Cheyenne in 1868 and was employed as manager of a furniture store.

Cheyenne had just become the terminal town of the new railroad. It was a wild and boisterous place where fists, and often guns, made the law. Warren saw the need for strong government, stable business concerns and the civilizing influences of the East to tame Cheyenne into a respectable city.

When he arrived, it had a reputation as the wide-open gambling center of the West, hardly the place for a calm-headed New Englander to build a firm future. Friends urged him to move on. Most of the transients who had come with the railroad boom did pull up stakes and head farther West as the rails reached beyond Cheyenne. But Warren made his own decision to stay and to cast his lot with the permanent settlers. He invested his money in Cheyenne's business enterprises and then reinvested in cattle.

In 1876 he married Helen Smith of Middlefield, Connecticut, and started the Warren ranch in the rolling meadowlands south of Cheyenne. Seven years later, when he formed the Warren Livestock Company to consolidate his cattle holdings, it was one of the largest cattle operations in the whole area.

Meanwhile, to bring Cheyenne better government, he served on the board of trustees, the city council and then as mayor. He got together a group of businessmen who formed a corporation to build an opera house. At its opening performance, special trains brought guests from Laramie, sixty miles away, and some culture seekers even came from as far away as Denver and other parts of Colorado.

Recognized as a leader of Wyoming's cattle industry, Warren didn't let the old prejudices stop him from investing in sheep ranches. In later years, the sheepmen hailed him as "the patriarch" of their industry. He became president of the National Wool Growers Association.

His interest in government had led to his election as a Senator in the territorial legislature and then to the post of treasurer of the territory. In 1885, President Chester A. Arthur appointed Warren territorial governor. Less than two years later, a change in national politics put him out of office, when a Democrat was appointed in his place.

The shift in the governorship, which came not because of the will of the people of Wyoming but because of a political change in far-off Washington, strengthened Warren's feeling that it was time for Wyoming to make a real fight for statehood. When Benjamin Harrison became President, he reappointed Warren territorial governor.

As governor, he moved at once to lead the territory to statehood. The people were behind him and Wyoming almost matched Idaho's speed in its orderly ratification of the state constitution. Just one week later than Idaho, on July 10, 1890, Wyoming entered the Union.

Warren became Wyoming's first elected governor and resigned to go to Washington as one of the state's first two Senators. For almost the next forty years, except for a two-year period when was he was out of office, Francis Warren was a Senator from Wyoming.

Representing the state that had first given women the right to vote, he was one of the champions of the equal suffrage amendment to the Constitution. He also was one of the leaders of the movement to obtain government assistance in irrigating dry farmlands. When he died in 1929, he was the last Union soldier still serving in Congress.

UTAH

Motto: Industry

Flower: Sego Lily

Bird: Seagull

Tree: Blue Spruce

Admitted to the Union: 1896

Utah was settled by the Mormons in 1847, a year before the land became part of the United States by treaty with Mexico. The Mormons asked to have the area admitted to the Union as the state of Deseret, but their government was not recognized by Congress. In 1850 Utah was organized as a territory and Brigham Young, leader of the Mormons, was named territorial governor.

In Utah, the Mormons hoped they would be able to establish a government in accord with their religion of the Church of the Latter-day Saints. Persecuted because of their beliefs and driven out of other colonies they had started in the East, they had traveled miles into a desolate land nobody wanted. As its first residents, they hoped to be free to govern as they chose.

But their prosperous farm settlements and the growing city of Salt Lake drew non-Mormon outsiders into the area. When gold was discovered in California, hundreds of adventurers came into Utah for supplies to carry them across the desert to the gold fields.

Many of the Easterners, as well as some of the appointed territorial officials, had little tolerance for the beliefs and customs of the Mormons. Sensational stories about marriages to more than one wife aroused strong anti-Mormon protests throughout the rest of the nation.

When Mormon leaders sought statehood in 1856, their bid was refused. Feeling was so strong that the Republican Party platform that year denounced plural marriages along with slavery as "the twin relics of barbarism." Exaggerated reports reached the East that the Mormons were in open rebellion against the Federal Government, and President Buchanan sent troops into Utah.

Open warfare was prevented by a truce between Mormon leaders and federal officials, but emotions were still so high on both sides that Utah had little chance of becoming a state. During the Civil War, federal troops were stationed in Utah because of Northern fears that it might throw its support to the Confederacy.

The Mormons re-established their own independent state of Deseret in 1861 and, each year for nine years, its legislature met and passed laws identical to those adopted by the recognized territorial government.

Meanwhile, with the opening of mines and the building of railroads, more and more non-Mormon settlers came to stay. They established a political party and gradually gained control in some parts of Utah. At the same time, the Federal Government waged a campaign against plural marriages. In 1890 the Church asked its members to give up the practice.

With the conditions that had long kept Utah from statehood finally changed, an enabling act was introduced into Congress in 1892 and Utah at last was admitted to the Union in 1896.

PATRICK CONNOR
(1820–1891)

Patrick Connor came to Utah in 1861 as the leader of federal troops prepared to fight the Mormons. He never did. Although he never really liked them, he grew to respect them and they found respect for him.

He was not a state maker in the usual sense. But he helped to change the conditions that kept Utah from statehood by encouraging non-Mormons to settle in the area and then by uniting them in a political party that broke the long deadlock between the Mormons and the Federal Government.

Born in County Kerry in Ireland, Patrick Connor was brought to New York by his parents while he was a young boy. The Connors were poor and there wasn't much chance for him to go to school. He was still just a boy when he started work as a laborer and when he was nineteen he joined the army.

He enlisted as a private and rose to the rank of captain during eight years of soldiering that led him into action against the Seminole Indians and into several battles of the Mexican War. When he quit the army, he set out to seek his fortune in the California gold fields. Although he had no luck in striking it rich, he did meet a pretty Irish girl from his native County Kerry and they were married in California in 1854.

When the Civil War began, Connor gave up his search for gold and re-enlisted in the army. He was made a colonel and put in command of the Military District of Utah. The reports were that the Mormons were in open rebellion and he set out with a force of three hundred volunteers to storm the territory and crush the revolt.

Much to his surprise, he discovered that the reports of open revolt were false. When he arrived in Salt Lake City, there were no Mormons to fight. Connor found the residents quietly going about their usual business. The Mormons simply turned their backs upon his men as Connor marched his troops through the streets to camp on a plateau overlooking the city.

Instead of fighting Mormons, he used his troops to help put down attacks by Indians against the settlers. His "war against the Mormons" became a different kind of campaign, aimed at breaking the control they had over the business and government of the area.

The Mormons were against mining, except to develop supplies of lead, iron and coal for their own needs. Connor, with the knowledge he had gained as a miner in California, set about encouraging mining in Utah as a way to bring in non-Mormon settlers.

He sent his troops out prospecting in the hills, searching for mineral wealth. People soon began calling the soldiers "Connor's Diggers." Anyone who found a bit of ore would bring it to Colonel Connor. The discoveries led to the opening of many new mines, some of them rated as among the richest silver and lead deposits in the world.

Connor gained nothing from the mines himself, except the satisfaction of opening them and creating both the excitement and the demand for men that brought hundreds of new non-Mormon settlers into the territory. Called Utah's "Father of Mining," he left the army in 1866 to take the political leadership that would pave the way for eventual statehood.

He organized the non-Mormons in what was known as the Liberal Political Party and became its head. The group had its headquarters in the town of Corinne, on the shore of the Great Salt Lake. At first it was a place that seemed doomed by bad luck. Business was threatened with failure because the railroad bypassed the town. Indians attacked it, epidemics swept it, and its farm crops were killed by alkali that worked its way up in the soil.

But despite hard luck, Corinne gradually prospered. Led by Connor, the town and its citizens formed the only organized resistance within the territory to the rule of the Church. As long as the Mormons held unchallenged political power in Utah, the Federal Government was not likely to listen favorably to appeals for recognition as a state. Connor's personal battle was against the Mormons, but in fighting them he managed to open the whole area to political change.

He built the first non-Mormon school, established a newspaper to express the views of the Liberal Party, owned the first steamboat on the Great Salt Lake. Meanwhile, the Federal Government carried on a constant campaign against Mormon policies that helped the Liberal Party gain strength.

In 1899 voters put the Liberals into power in the city of Ogden and, the next year, in Salt Lake City itself. Church leaders then dissolved the Mormon political party and urged its members to vote within the national Democratic and Republican parties.

At the age of seventy-one, in December 1891, just before the bill was introduced to enable Utah to become a state, Patrick Connor died. He had given the Mormons no reason to like him, but he had earned their respect, as well as that of his own followers who mourned the death of the "liberator" who helped make statehood possible.

OKLAHOMA

Motto: Labor Conquers All Things

Flower: Mistletoe   Bird: Scissor-tailed Flycatcher

Tree: Redbud

Admitted to the Union: 1907

☆

Most of what is now Oklahoma was bought by the United States as part of the Louisiana Purchase. The land was chosen to be the home of Indians from the Gulf states when they were moved west of the Mississippi River after 1820. Each of what were known as the Five Civilized Tribes was a small Indian republic with constitutional laws and other regulations to keep order.

During the Civil War, most of the Indians sympathized with the South. When the war ended, the Five Civilized Tribes signed a separate peace treaty with the United States. They were forced to sell half their lands to the government for a very small sum of money as a penalty for supporting the Confederacy.

Homesteaders tried to move into part of the area not assigned to any Indian tribe, claiming that it was public land which should be open to settlement. A group of would-be settlers, organized in 1880 by David L. Payne, became known as "boomers." They made many attempts to establish homes in the region, returning again and again, even though they were moved out each time by federal troops.

Finally, Congress decided to open some two million acres to settlement. High noon of April 22, 1889, was set as the time, and fifty thousand people gathered to rush into the lands to claim homesteads. Other parts of the western Indian reservations were opened to settlers in the same way. Some people managed to get inside the boundaries before the crowds rushed in, and those who sneaked in sooner than the legal starting time for the land runs became known as "sooners."

Meanwhile the eastern half of the Indian lands was still held and governed by the Five Civilized Tribes. It was an area barred to American settlers and beyond the reach of federal law enforcement, and became a haven for outlaws and other fugitives who fled there to escape punishment.

The western section was organized as Oklahoma Territory in 1891. But the Indians in the eastern part, where the Five Tribes already had their own governments, were against being joined to the western part at first. They wanted to be admitted to the Union as a separate Indian state. A convention was called in 1905 to frame a constitution and to petition Congress to admit the Indian state of Sequoyah.

Congress refused and insisted that the two territories be combined. An enabling act was passed to permit delegates from both territories to form a joint constitution. They met in convention in November 1906 and the constitution they wrote was quickly approved by the people and accepted by Congress. Oklahoma, combining both Indian territories, was admitted to the Union one year later.

CHARLES HASKELL
(1860–1933)

Charles Haskell just about brought the twentieth century with him to Oklahoma. It was the first year of the new century when he arrived in what was the Indian Territory. He built railroads across it and telephone lines to bring people closer together, and then helped to build a state of the lands he crossed by bringing together the two political halves of Oklahoma.

He was a schoolteacher, lawyer, investor and businessman who made nearly as many enemies as he made friends. Haskell earned and lost several fortunes, took chances that sometimes left him nearly penniless, built big companies, went broke and borrowed money to make himself a millionaire, and then lost it all again. But he helped shape raw Western villages toward becoming modern towns and cities and took the leadership of the first state government.

Born in Ohio the year before the Civil War began, he was the youngest of six children. His father died when he was only three and although his widowed mother struggled for a time to keep the family together, he finally was sent to live with a neighboring schoolteacher. Haskell managed to get through elementary school, but the rest of his education was self-learned from borrowed books.

He taught himself so well that he qualified for a teacher's certificate when he was seventeen. For several years he was the teen-aged schoolmaster of one-room country schools where some of his students were nearly as old and as big as he was. While he was teaching classes by day, he taught himself law at night.

Admitted to the bar in 1880, he opened a law office in the town of Ottawa, Ohio. It was the midst of the railroad building boom and, as a lawyer, he had a chance to become interested in the organization of several railroad companies. Soon he was organizing companies of his own and constructing short-line routes that crisscrossed Ohio and led into nearby states to connect main lines.

The then still newly invented telephone also was pushing its lines westward. Haskell, always a man with enthusiasm for things that were new, became a telephone pioneer. He brought the first telephones to several parts of Ohio and in 1900 went to Texas to establish companies there. But he was in Texas hardly a year when a new frontier quickened his interest.

Railroads were building across the Indian Territory and he wanted to help build them. Haskell moved to Muskogee, then still a Wild West town in an area beyond the control of federal law. He had a part in building two rail lines across the Indian lands and later brought streetcars to Muskogee. Settling down to become one of its leading citizens, he established a bank and built a hotel.

Lawlessness grew along the path of the rail lines, in the tent towns and temporary settlements that sprang up where the railroads were being constructed. Even in some of the more permanent towns, men did just about as they pleased. As a lawyer and a businessman, Haskell recognized the need for better government. He became a leader of the statehood movement.

The Indian tribes and many of the settlers of the eastern area wanted it to become a separate state. Haskell was chosen a delegate in 1905 to the convention that met to write a constitution for the proposed state of Sequoyah. Almost everybody in the area was in favor of it, but Congress refused to accept the Indian Territory as a state unless it was joined by the western half, the Oklahoma Territory.

The movement for statehood was less organized in the western section, where homesteaders had rushed in to claim lands after years of struggling with the Federal Government for the right to settle upon them. But Congress passed the act to enable delegates from both regions to consider becoming a state and the joint convention was called.

When it met in 1906, Haskell was made floor leader for the Democratic Party. He proved his leadership by drawing together the opposing factions. Haskell showed such clear ability for organizing the convention activities that when the new state finally was formed, he was elected its first governor by a large majority.

It was a state big in size, newly rich, heavily populated by people who hadn't been there long. His task as governor lay in pulling together both territories into one strong state. Haskell neglected his own personal affairs and even his health to devote himself to the job. By the time his term of office was over, he was ill and in financial difficulties.

Friends saw to it that he had enough funds to allow him to rest and regain his health. Within a few years, Haskell was again building railroads, toll roads, oil and gas companies and his own great fortune. He became a millionaire and then, once more, lost nearly everything in the stock market crash of 1929. Four years later, Haskell died at age seventy-three.

NEW MEXICO

Motto: It Grows as It Goes

Flower: Yucca   Bird: Road Runner

Tree: Piñon

Admitted to the Union: 1912

☆

When Mexico became independent from Spain in 1821, New Mexico was opened to trade with the United States. The first wagons loaded with goods from Missouri crossed the plains the next year to establish the historic Santa Fe Trail.

During the war with Mexico, which began in 1846, New Mexico was declared part of the United States and its government came under military control. The treaty that ended the war called for admitting New Mexico to the United States "at the proper time." But New Mexicans had to wait another sixty-four years for statehood.

A convention of delegates met at Santa Fe in 1848 and petitioned Congress for speedy organization of civil territorial government, but the petition was refused. The next year, they sent a delegate to Congress, but he was denied a seat. In 1850 a convention framed a constitution for the proposed "State of New Mexico." The people approved it and a legislature met and elected United States Senators.

Congress turned down the bid for statehood and offered a compromise instead, under which New Mexico became a territory with full civil government. The act also settled land claims made by Texas and, in 1853, additional territory was bought from Mexico.

New Mexico, occupied by Southern forces, briefly was proclaimed part of the Confederate States during the Civil War until control was recaptured by Union troops. Indians took advantage of the situation to attack settlers and Colonel Kit Carson was sent to help subdue them. In 1876 a feud involving rival cattlemen broke into open warfare. The dispute, called the Lincoln County War, forced the calling out of federal troops, but it ended before the soldiers were brought into action.

Meanwhile the mining industry had developed, mail and telegraph services had quickened communication with the East, and the great cattle ranches soon were to give way to the growth of farming with the coming of railroads that replaced the stagecoach lines and wagon freight trails.

The first "iron horse" huffed into New Mexico in 1878 to increase the cattle boom for a time and to bring in modern machinery for the mines. The railroads carried hundreds of new settlers, and irrigation projects helped them turn arid land into flourishing farms. But the move for statehood again was delayed by the nation's declaration of war against Spain.

In 1906 joint statehood with Arizona failed when the people of Arizona voted against it. However, four years later, Congress finally passed an enabling act to admit New Mexico and Arizona as separate states, after each had adopted state constitutions. New Mexico quickly called a convention and a constitution was adopted in 1911. But Congress asked for changes in it, which delayed New Mexico's admission until the following year.

GEORGE CURRY

(1863–1947)

George Curry grew up with New Mexico. Born in Louisiana two years after the outbreak of the Civil War, he lived until two years after the end of the Second World War. From the time he was in his teens, he was part of the changing life of New Mexico, a cowboy who moved to the governor's mansion and to a seat in Congress as spokesman for the new state he helped bring into the Union.

He was fourteen when he first came to the territory of New Mexico to settle in Lincoln County, where a feud between a cattle king and smaller ranchers over land and water rights became a war in which both groups hired gunmen to shoot it out. Pitched battles were staged in the town of Lincoln, men were murdered in the hills, and more than a score of killings were counted before the Federal Government restored order.

The range war had just ended when George Curry started work as a ranch hand. Still in his teens, he helped to round up cattle and deliver them to market. For a time he worked in the store at Fort Stanton, an isolated outpost where he traded with the Indians. He went into business for himself, with a store of his own, and became interested in politics.

He was twenty-three when he became deputy treasurer of Lincoln County. The next year, he was made county clerk. By then, the last of New Mexico's fierce Indian tribes had surrendered and the Santa Fe Trail, a major trade route for sixty years, was giving way to the railroads. Times were changing, the great cattle empires were gradually being replaced by farms, and the towns were growing with new settlers who renewed the demand for statehood.

Chosen sheriff in 1892, he served as a Western lawman who helped to bring orderly government to the area. Two years later, Curry was first elected to the territorial senate. Active in the continuing struggle for statehood, he became president of the senate in 1896.

But he put aside his own political career at the outbreak of the war with Spain in 1898 and was among the first to volunteer to serve with the famed Rough Riders under Theodore Roosevelt. Curry soon became a captain of the victorious American forces. Mustered out of service, he returned for a few months to New Mexico and was made sheriff of Otero County.

He gave up his job as sheriff to volunteer for duty with American troops occupying the Philippine Islands, and it was there that he gained the experience which was to lead him to the governorship of New Mexico. During the seven years he was in the Philippines, he organized the first police force in the city of Manila, acted as its head, and then served as governor of three of the island provinces.

Both Roosevelt, who had been his leader when Curry was a Rough Rider, and William Howard Taft, who was civil governor of the Philippines, recognized Curry's ability. Roosevelt called him back to New Mexico in 1907 to become territorial governor. New Mexico's bid for joint statehood with Arizona had just failed.

As governor of the territory, Curry took command of the fight to make it a separate state. He was governor during the four years that finally led to the convention which framed the state constitution. The bill to make New Mexico a state was signed by Curry's former boss in the Philippines, Taft, who by then had become President.

When New Mexico was admitted to the Union, George Curry was elected its first Congressman. He declined to run for re-election after his first term and settled down at the age of fifty to operate a hotel.

His days of public service were not over. In the First World War he was a member of the Council of National Defense. Later, he was called upon to help determine the border between the United States and Mexico. Once again he retired, this time to a ranch near Cutter. But in the Second World War, he served as chairman of a county draft board.

After the war, George Curry became State Historian, helping to preserve the records and the history of the state he had helped to create. He was historian for two years before his death at Albuquerque in 1947.

ARIZONA

Motto: God Enriches

Flower: Saguaro Cactus Flower

Bird: Cactus Wren

Tree: Paloverde

Admitted to the Union: 1912

☆

Under Spanish and Mexican rule and in the early American territorial days, Arizona was part of New Mexico. During the Civil War, residents of the region near the Mexican border declared their sympathies with the South and Jefferson Davis proclaimed Arizona a territory of the Confederacy.

In 1863 the United States Congress established a separate territory of Arizona. Population grew steadily during the years that followed, despite Indian raids that continued until the death of Geronimo in 1886. Rich silver and copper mines, as well as the building of railroads, were strong attractions for settlers.

The first move for statehood was approved by the House of Representatives in 1892, but was defeated in the Senate. Ten years later, a senatorial committee on statehood approved a plan for the admission of New Mexico and Arizona as a single state. Arizona's Congressional delegate made an impassioned plea against this plan to combine both areas in one state. Voters in Arizona overwhelmingly defeated the measure and held out for independent statehood.

In 1910 the enabling act for the formation of two separate states was passed. Arizona was admitted to the Union one month after New Mexico, February 14, 1912—forty-nine years after it had been made a territory.

GEORGE HUNT
(1859–1934)

George Hunt was without a dollar in his pocket when he rode into Globe, Arizona, in 1881 on the back of a pack mule. It was a raw new town, defiantly built in the heart of Apache Indian territory by silver-seeking miners. The surface silver of the mines had just about run out and Hunt found work for a time as a waiter in a Chinese restaurant.

Then rich copper ore was discovered beneath the silver and he got a job with the Old Dominion Copper Company, shoveling muck in underground tunnels where the air was so foul miners could hardly keep their work candles lighted. It was dangerous, backbreaking labor, sweating out his strength for long hours in the dark passages where every day's work was a threat to health and safety.

For the next fifty years, George Hunt was a champion of the men who worked the mines. He fought for better labor laws and a government that would back them. Hunt organized the vote of the miners behind the drive to bring separate statehood to Arizona.

Born in Huntsville, Missouri, in 1859, he was the son of a prosperous landowner who had gone to California himself in the gold rush days of the '49ers. As a boy, he listened to his father's tales of the mines and grew up with a yearning for adventure of his own. His mother, Sarah Yates Hunt, was a writer for women's magazines of the time. When George was nineteen, he left home and bummed his way to Colorado, riding the rails.

He worked at whatever odd jobs he could find to give himself a stake for prospecting all through the Colorado mining country. Without any luck at striking it rich, he wandered from Pueblo to Denver, from Golden to Leadville and Gunnison. But he learned about mines and the men who worked them, shared their hardships and won their friendship.

When his funds ran out completely, he wandered south-ward into New Mexico and signed on as a construction hand to help spike the ties and lay the rails of the new Atchison, Topeka and Sante Fe Railroad. His youthful thirst for adventure still was not satisfied, he joined a group of other young men and floated down the Rio Grande on a flatboat. At El Paso, he quit his companions to head west on his own again.

His drifting took him through Deming and Lordsburg and into the mining town of Globe, astride the mule that carried all his belongings in a single tattered pack. As a laborer in the mines of Globe, George Hunt became a popular figure among the men whose work he shared, and businessmen in the community also began to take notice of him.

They recognized his popularity and the way he had of getting along with the miners, and he soon had an office job with the Old Dominion Commercial Company. By the time he was forty, he was the company's president. Hunt acquired a ranch on the Salt River and entered politics. He served as the first mayor of Globe and as county treasurer.

His real start in politics, as a friend and supporter of labor, came mostly through the backing he received from the workers of Globe who had organized the territory's first and strongest miners' union. Elected a member of the territorial legislature in 1892, he served in both houses for a total of eight years during the time when the first bids for statehood were being made.

Although he was out of office for a few years after that, Hunt was chosen delegate to the Democratic National Convention at Kansas City that nominated William J. Bryan for President in 1900. In 1904, the year he married Helen Ellison, he once again was elected to the upper house of the territorial legislature, where he served another six years, twice as president of the council.

As a leader of the battle for independent statehood, he helped to fight the proposal that would have combined Arizona with New Mexico in a single state. Throughout his terms, he also sponsored many legislative acts to improve working conditions in Arizona, proving again his friendship for the labor group that strengthened his hand in the struggle to make Arizona a separate state.

By the time Congress finally passed the enabling act in 1910, authorizing Arizona to frame a constitution, Hunt was a man in his fifties, a dignified, solidly built individual with a flowing moustache and a firm and determined manner. But the miners hadn't forgotten that he had labored as one of them. He persuaded the aggressive unions in the territory that they could share in the making of the constitution for the new state only by putting their vote solidly behind his Democratic Party.

The election battle was a lively one, but Hunt was chosen among the fifty-two delegates who met in Phoenix in October to write the constitution. He was named president of the convention and guided it through a stormy path of debate toward final statehood. The sessions lasted two months and became a seesaw battle between labor and conservative groups. Through his influence, agreement was reached at last.

George Hunt was elected Arizona's first state governor the following year and was re-elected for two more terms. After his third term, he retired to live quietly for a few years in Phoenix. President Wilson named him Minister to Siam in 1920, but Hunt resigned the following year to run once more for the governorship. Twice again, he was re-elected to serve his fifth and then sixth terms.

He built a powerful political organization, but by the end of his sixth term as governor he was at odds with the legislature. Opponents accused him of running a political machine. In 1928 a Republican defeated him for office, but two years later the people voted George Hunt in for the seventh and last time as the chief of Arizona's government.

Some of those who had loyally supported him turned against him bitterly and the tide of changing politics ended his popularity. Finally, in his seventies, he retired completely from public office. Hated by some and still idolized by others, an almost legendary figure of the Southwest, he died at his Phoenix home in 1934, acclaimed by his friends as the Father of Statehood for Arizona.

ALASKA

Flower: Forget-me-not   Bird: Willow Ptarmigan

Admitted to the Union: 1959

☆

When the United States bought Alaska from Russia just after the Civil War, few Americans realized it was the biggest land bargain since the Louisiana Purchase. The treaty, arranged by Secretary of State William Seward, barely managed to win Senate approval and was denounced as "Seward's Folly" by those who considered Alaska nothing but an icy wasteland.

During the first thirty years under the American flag, the homestead and general land laws did not apply to Alaska. Fifteen bills introduced to give Alaska civil government were ignored by Congress. Alaska was pretty much a forgotten land, five thousand miles away from the concerns of the government in Washington.

Suddenly the news burst upon the nation that gold had been found. The Klondike discovery of 1897 brought a stampede of sixty thousand fortune seekers into Alaska and captured the whole country's romantic sense of adventure. Many of those who failed to find gold discovered Alaska's greater riches of timber, fish and coal. Others stayed to hunt or to farm, to build homes and settlements.

They renewed their demands for self-government. In 1906 Alaska was allowed to send a non-voting delegate to Congress. Six years later, it became a territory with the right to elect its own legislature. In 1916 the first bill for statehood was introduced.

The bill got nowhere. The battle for self-government had just begun. Making Alaska a state would mean taking into the

Union a far-distant land, separated by British Canada, and the opposition was strong. A hundred reasons were found for denying statehood, some inspired by commercial interests that enjoyed a freedom in Alaska they would lose if it became a state.

It took the Second World War and the threat of Japanese invasion to make the nation really aware of Alaska's importance. Military establishments also brought roads, housing, airfields and land surveys.

Radio and other modern communications already had lessened Alaska's isolation. Increased air travel brought Alaska still closer. In 1946 Alaskans voted three to two in favor of statehood. But it was twelve years more before Alaska finally was admitted to the Union, after ninety-one years of hoping to become a state.

ERNEST GRUENING
(1887–   )

He was a boy of eleven when Alaska first captured his imagination. A boy who lived in New York, a whole continent away. But the books he read, the talk he heard, the newspapers he saw, were filled with the excitement of the fabulous Klondike gold discovery.

Clerks and bankers, actresses and scrubwomen, people of all kinds and all ages, in San Francisco and New York and in the whole country between, dropped whatever they were doing and headed by the thousands aboard any craft that would float them toward the romantic places named Dawson, Skagway and Nome.

It was 1898, and the year before, the S.S. *Portland* had docked at Seattle with "a ton of gold." Alaska had become the new frontier of adventure. Like most boys his age, Ernest Gruening dreamed of being an Alaskan prospector. Excitedly he told his parents he would go to Alaska when he was old enough, and would make his fame and fortune there.

Perhaps they smiled indulgently, as parents will over boyish dreams of adventure in far-off lands. Certainly they never guessed, any more than he did at the time, that he would one day serve as Alaska's governor, champion of its fight for statehood, and first Senator.

"My parents took a dim view of a prospecting career for an eleven-year-old and that career died a-borning," he said in later years, recalling that boyhood touch of gold fever. "I was to see Alaska, but not until a medical education and a newspaper career had put nearly forty more years behind me."

Sent to a private school in Connecticut, he went on to Harvard and to his medical studies in Boston. Although he received his degree as a doctor, his talent with words and ideas had a stronger pull upon him. He gave up his career in medicine to go into journalism. Starting as a reporter and then a rewrite man, he worked his way up through the news rooms of various Boston papers to become a city editor and a managing editor.

Moving to New York, he became managing editor of two papers there and also edited a national magazine. Later on, he started a newspaper of his own in Portland, Maine. Through his newspaper and article writing, Gruening developed a special interest in Latin America, Mexico and other lands that bordered on the United States.

His studies and travels in Mexico and the book he wrote about them led to his appointment in 1933 as an adviser to the United States delegations at the Inter-American conference in Montevideo. The next year, President Roosevelt invited him to head a new federal agency, the Division of Territories and Island Possessions. Working under the Department of the Interior, Gruening took charge of supervising relations with all the American possessions outside the United States, including Alaska.

It was during his five years as director of the agency that he finally made his first visits to the land of his boyhood dreams. In the spring of 1936, when he first saw Alaska, there was no airline or highway to link it to the United States. He made the voyage by steamer up the Inside Passage, a thousand miles of sheltered waterway from Puget Sound to Skagway.

Despite all he had read, he was surprised by the majestic loneliness of mile after mile of forests and glaciers. "Only an occasional thread of smoke from a cabin betrayed human life," he wrote. "I felt as if I had stepped back fifty years into American history."

As he became familiar with Alaska's problems, Gruening discovered that Alaska's government also was something of a political relic of the past. He felt that Alaska had suffered for years, as he later put it, from "congressional policies and bureaucratic tyranny unparalleled in any other territory," which thwarted its natural development.

Three years after that first visit, he was appointed in 1939 as governor of Alaska. It was the start of more than thirteen years' service in that position, the longest of any governor in Alaska's history. Three times, the President appointed him to four-year terms and each time the United States Senate voted its unanimous approval.

With his long experience as a newspaperman, editor, writer and federal administrator, he was a man who knew his way in national politics as well as in matters of government, and who also knew how to put Alaska's hope of statehood into words that would be heard and understood.

Physically a vital and energetic man, he was the first Alaskan governor to visit all the territory's outlying settlements. Heavy-set, square-jawed, with a prominent nose and a ready grin, he once was described as "suave in manner, with composure unshakable, but a slugger in a fight" when it came to gaining political advantage. As the leader of Alaska's fight for statehood, Gruening kept up the battle through years of disappointment and near victory.

Many of the arguments raised against statehood were almost the same as those made against admitting the earlier territories that became states. Opponents said that Alaska wasn't connected with the rest of the continental United States, that it was too far away, that its population was too small, that it couldn't afford the tax burden of state government.

Alaskans answered that when California was admitted in 1850, miles of mountains and wilderness separated it from the nearest state. They claimed that radio, telephone, telegraph and the airplane actually had put Alaska much nearer to Washington in travel time and communication than Boston was from New York when the Union was formed. They declared that other territories had less population when they became states and that the added cost of state government could be met by the increased revenues the state would get.

The statehood bill introduced in 1943 brought no action from Congress. Two years later, Alaska's legislature requested admission as a state and called for a referendum the following year so the people could vote on the question. Alaskans voted three to two for statehood. In 1956 they voted for a proposed state constitution.

Presidents and the national political parties favored statehood for Alaska. Four times, Congressional committees approved. Once the bill actually passed the House. Another time, statehood was defeated by one vote in the Senate.

Finally, forty-two years after the first official request for statehood, the decisive vote came. On the evening of June 30, 1958, after six days of heated debate, the roll was called in the United States Senate chamber. Gruening and those with him in the long battle waited in the Senate gallery. The House had given its approval a month before.

One by one, the Senators called out their decision, sixty-four of them in favor of statehood and twenty against, and the Senate's presiding officer announced, "So the bill has passed." In the galleries the supporters of statehood broke the Senate custom of strict silence and burst into cheering and applause. "My own hands ached from their part in it," Gruening said.

The joyful news was flashed to Alaska, where jubilant citizens sent up balloons and tried to dye a river gold. Church bells rang, sirens howled, stores were shut and people paraded into the streets as parties and celebrations lasted through the night. In the Senate in Washington, Gruening and the others went to the chapel and offered a prayer.

On the morning of January 3, 1959, President Eisenhower signed the proclamation admitting Alaska as the forty-ninth state. In Alaska, the people voted their own approval, and elected Ernest Gruening, champion of statehood, as one of their first two Senators.

HAWAII

Motto: The Life of the Land Is Perpetuated in Righteousness
Flower: Hibiscus   Bird: Hawaiian Goose
Tree: Candlenut
Admitted to the Union: 1959

☆

Separated from the mainland by more than 2,000 miles of the Pacific Ocean, Hawaii was a monarchy, republic and territory before it became a state.

Chief Kamehameha, called "the Napoleon of the Pacific," brought all the islands under his rule in 1795. He and his descendants reigned for a century before Hawaii became a territory of the United States.

The first king's son, Kamehameha II, kept Britain or Russia from annexing his islands and in 1820 received the first agent to represent a foreign government in Hawaii, American John C. Jones, Jr. The next Hawaiian monarch, Kamehameha III, gave the people a voice in the government by granting them their first written constitution in 1840. Hawaii might have been annexed to the United States during his reign, if his death in 1854 hadn't prevented the signing of the treaty.

Hawaii was governed by two more Kamehamehas and when the throne was left vacant in 1873, Prince William Lunalilo appealed to the people to choose their own ruler and was elected king by popular vote. Hawaiian monarchy ended in 1893 when Queen Liliuokalani was dethroned. The Republic of Hawaii was formed, with the son of an American missionary, Sanford B. Dole, as president.

Dole became first governor of the territory of Hawaii after

it was annexed by the United States, with his help, in 1898. Hawaii's initial bid for statehood was made to Congress in 1903. But it was eighteen years more before the first bill for Hawaiian statehood was introduced in Congress.

The territorial legislature called a state convention to write a constitution in 1950 and the people voted in favor of adopting it. After Alaska achieved statehood, new attempts were made to bring Hawaii into the Union and it finally became the fiftieth of the United States in 1959.

WALLACE FARRINGTON
(1871–1933)

Wallace Farrington, a territorial governor of Hawaii, was a pioneer advocate of statehood. His son, Joseph, followed in his footsteps and became Hawaii's longtime statehood champion in Congress. When Joseph died at his desk in Washington, the battle for statehood was carried on by his widow, Elizabeth Farrington.

Queen Liliuokalani had just been overthrown and the Hawaiian Republic formed when Wallace Farrington first came to the Islands in 1894 as a young man in his twenties. Born in Maine, he had gone to college there and then had become a newspaper reporter. Hired by a Honolulu paper, he wrote eyewitness reports of Hawaii's revolt for freedom.

Hawaii, even then, sought to be annexed as a state. When President Grover Cleveland withdrew the annexation treaty and tried to restore the queen to her throne, Hawaiians revolted and set up the republic, forcing the queen to renounce her claims.

The start of the Spanish-American War in 1898 made Honolulu a mid-Pacific food and fuel supply port for United States ships on their way to the Philippines. Farrington, as a working reporter, covered the news of those eventful years and wrote of the strategic importance of the Islands. He was among those who encouraged the annexation, finally approved in August 1898.

Under the agreement, Hawaii was to be made "an integral part" of the United States. Farrington and his son later argued that the annexation treaty itself was a promise that the United States eventually would grant statehood to Hawaii, as it did to Texas, the only other territory annexed under such terms.

After the act that made Hawaii a territory was signed into law in 1900, Farrington took a leading part in helping to organize the political party that sent Prince Kuhio, a nephew of the former queen, to Congress as Hawaii's non-voting representative. Popularly known as "Prince Cupid," Kuhio served Hawaii in Washington for the next twenty years.

Farrington, as a strong supporter of statehood, helped influence the new legislature to make its first formal bid for admission as a state in 1903. But the petition was ignored by Congress, as were the new petitions sent by almost every legislature that followed. The fight to become a state settled down to an organized campaign.

In the newspaper of which he had become editor and part owner, in the merchants' association he headed, and as an influential figure in other civic affairs, Farrington helped to keep alive the enthusiasm for statehood, despite Washington's reluctance to act.

President Harding, in 1921, named him governor of the territory. For eighteen years, Hawaii had been presenting Congress with the territory's rights and needs without much recognition. As governor, Farrington officially called the attention of the Secretary of the Interior to the fact that the United States received large sums of money from Hawaii in taxes every year, but gave very little in return. Congress left it out of the general appropriations for such things as education, good roads and farm loans.

Farrington's appeal was, in effect, an echo of the old cry of the nation's founding fathers against "taxation without representation." Following his lead, the Hawaiian legislature of 1923 adopted a Bill of Rights. The bill retold the history of Hawaii's annexation and clearly set forth the reasons why Hawaii should be treated as a state.

Farrington took the Bill of Rights to Washington and devoted himself to the task of getting federal action on it. The bill served as the basis of a measure President Coolidge signed into law in 1924, granting Hawaii government aid. Coolidge reappointed Farrington governor the next year, giving him the honor of being the first Hawaiian chief executive to succeed himself in office.

Meanwhile, his son Joseph also was becoming a newspaperman and a fighter for Hawaiian statehood. Starting as a reporter in Philadelphia, Joseph became a Washington correspondent, served as a lieutenant in the First World War, and then was an editor of his father's Honolulu paper.

In 1932, the year before Wallace Farrington died, Joseph was Secretary of the Hawaiian Legislative Commission. Two years later, he became a member of the Hawaiian Senate. He gave his full support to the move to renew the appeal for a place in the Union.

Finally, after three decades of trying, Hawaii managed in 1935 to get a Congressional committee to hold its first public hearings on the issue. The hearings were followed by the appointment of a joint committee of Senators and Representatives to make an on-the-spot study. The committee suggested that the people should vote their feelings.

The vote was called for by the legislature in the territorial balloting of 1940 and 67 percent of Hawaii's voters answered "yes" to the question: "Do you favor statehood?" Hawaii expected Congress to accept the favorable decision as a mandate to grant immediate statehood. But Washington still was in no hurry to act.

The Japanese attack on Pearl Harbor, December 7, 1941, and the war that followed centered attention on Hawaii's importance as never before. The war brought many changes, but one thing that did not change, but became even stronger during the war years was Hawaii's deep desire for statehood. Joseph Farrington was first elected Hawaii's delegate to Congress in 1942 and dedicated himself, from that moment, to the cause of finally bringing about the long-delayed decision.

In 1947 the House of Representatives passed the Farrington bill to admit Hawaii into the union, but the bill failed the next year in the Senate. Despite the setback, Hawaii's voters in 1950 elected delegates to a convention that framed a state constitution. Twice more, in 1950 and again in 1953, Hawaiian statehood passed the House, but failed in the Senate. Hawaii and Alaska then were linked together for statehood in a single bill that was approved by the Senate, but not by the House.

While fighting for this bill's approval, in June 1954, Hawaii's six-term delegate and great statehood champion, Joseph Farrington, died. His widow was chosen to carry on the fight and served in Congress until defeated for re-election in 1956. By then, twenty-four hearings had been held on Hawaii's claims for admission, hundreds of witnesses had been heard, and the printed House and Senate reports on the subject over the years added up to seven thousand pages of testimony.

The victory, for which Wallace and Joseph Farrington had paved the way but which they didn't live to see, came at last on March 12, 1959. The bill already had gone through the Senate when the House met at noon that day. Three hours later the roll call started.

Hawaii's supporters nervously sat in the gallery, mentally counting up the votes. Before the final total of 323 to 89 was reached, the joyous news of victory was flashed over telephone lines held open to Honolulu.

In Washington, the advocates of statehood had been hopeful, but the sudden dramatic happy ending to the half century of other hopes and promises left them stunned. It was hard for them to believe. But within minutes, the wail of sirens, the peal of church bells, the whistles of ships, and the shouting of crowds in the streets of Honolulu celebrated what was fact.

President Eisenhower, on March 18 in a ceremony at the White House, signed the Hawaiian statehood bill into law.

The United States had become fifty.

INDEX

255

THE AUTHORS

Bill and Sue Severn have shared careers in writing and editing for some years. Together or separately, they have written eleven other books for young people, including *Magic and Magicians, Let's Give a Show,* and *Highways to Tomorrow,* as well as many short stories and articles.

In addition to free-lance writer, Bill Severn's occupations have included news editor for a national press association, reporter, radio executive, and newspaper advertising manager. Sue Severn has been a trade magazine editor and a newspaper correspondent, in addition to her free-lance writing assignments. The Severns make their home in Sheffield, Massachusetts.